D0075669

PLEASE NOTE:

This book contains graphic description of inhuman acts committed by a small but unfortunately significant segment of the Serb nation. It is published for the information of politicians, diplomats, historians, soldiers, reporters and other professionals. Not recommended to the general public.

To keep one's sanity it should be read with total professional detachment.

Please read POSTSCRIPTUM on page 162 **before** you start reading the book. It will give you basic knowledge and better understanding of the true nature of the Partisan Warfare.

The Publisher

TITOIST ATROCITIES
in
VOJVODINA 1944-1945

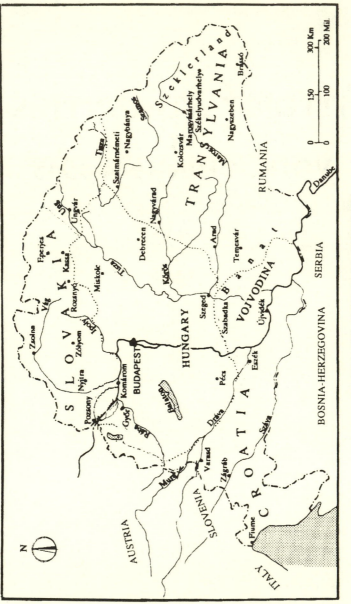

VOJVODINA IN CENTRAL-EUROPE

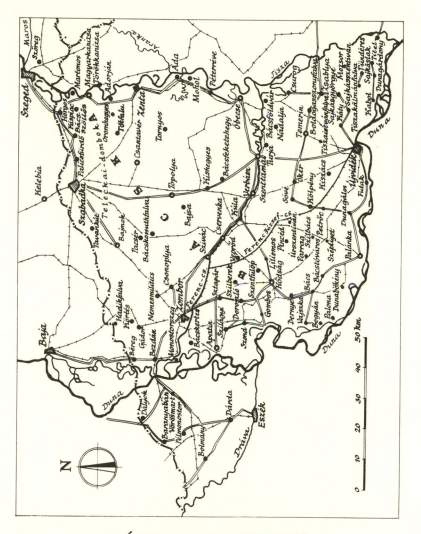

BÁCSKA (VOJVODINA)
WITH HUNGARIAN GEOGRAPHICAL NAMES

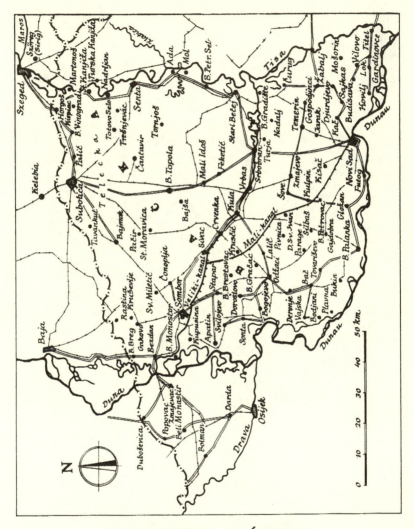

VOJVODINA (BÁCSKA)
WITH SERBIAN GEOGRAPHICAL NAMES

TITOIST ATROCITIES

in

VOJVODINA 1944-1945

SERBIAN VENDETTA IN BÁCSKA

TIBOR CSERES

HUNYADI PUBLISHING

WITHDRAWN
LVC BISHOP LIBRARY

Copyright ©1993 Tibor Cseres

All rights reserved

First edition in the English Language

Hunyadi Publishing
Buffalo, NY : Toronto, Ont.

Hungarian title: VÉRBOSSZÚ BÁCSKÁBAN

Library of Congress Catalogue Card Number 92-76218

ISBN 1-882785-01-0

Manufactured in the United States of America

WITHDRAWN
LVC BISHOP LIBRARY

334190

D
804
.Y8
C7613
1993

AUTHOR'S PREFACE TO THE ENGLISH EDITION

At the end of World War I, the southern part of the thousand year old historical Hungary was occupied by Serbian troops. Under the terms of the Paris Peace Treaty in 1921 it was annexed to the Serbo-Croat-Slovenian Kingdom, that later became Yugoslavia. The new name of this territory, situated to the east of present Croatia, was VOJVODINA (also spelled Voivodina or Voyvodina). Its former Hungarian name had been Bácska and Bánát.

During World War II, in 1941, Germany occupied Yugoslavia. At the same time, Hungary took possession of and re-annexed VOJVODINA from divided Yugoslavia. At the end of 1944, the Serbs reoccupied Bácska, which has belonged to Serbia ever since.

During the German occupation, a strong Serbian partisan movement developed with Communist leadership, which also spread over to Bácska, reannexed to Hungary at the time. The Hungarian military leadership organized anti-partisan raids and summary courts-martial against the participants in and sympathizers with the partisan movement. The biggest anti-partisan campaign took place in and around Novi Sad, in Hungarian, Ujvidék, where several hundred individuals suspected to be partisans, among them innocent people as well , were arrested and executed in the course of a three-day raid in January 1942. Although the army of every country treats partisans the same way, law-abiding Hungarian public opinion condemned the military leadership for the harsh action. Miklós Horthy, regent of Hungary, ordered an investigation against the organizers of the campaign. It is probably a unique incident in world history that a belligerent nation calls its own army to account for transgressions against the enemy. In my novel Cold Days, written in 1960, I related the story of the atrocities committed in Novi Sad in order to clear our consciences by sincerely revealing our own mistakes.

The three **"Cold Days"** were followed by **"freezing weeks"** in the whole territory of VOJVODINA in 1944, when the Serbians brutally massacred 40,000 Hungarian civilians, the overwhelming majority of them innocent beyond any doubt, in

revenge of the execution of 3,000 suspected Szerbian partisans.
. The commander-in-chief of the partisan army, Marshal Tito, as far as we know, did not give any expressed written command to butcher the Hungarians in Bácska. He did condon and apparently orally directed his partisans in the whole territory of Yugoslavia - including Vojvodina - to revenge all "injustices" suffered by partisans and Serbians during the four years of the war. In other words, where a stream of blood flowed in 1942, a torrent of blood should gush in 1944.

In the course' of the partisans three-year struggle for self-defence against the Nazis, but mainly against royalist chetniks and independence seeking Croats, homicidal traditions smouldering under the ashes ever since the Middle Ages were revived, enriching the various manners of death with numerous cruel novelties. While the Hungarian military justice executed the condemned one by one, the Serbian partisans bound ten or fifteen people with wire and killed them with a round of firearms. They had lined them up in front of the previously dug common graves so that they would only have to bury them with the earth that they themselves had dug from the pit. Whereas the sentence of Hungarian summary courts was hanging or shooting, the Serbian partisans killed their victims after various forms of torture. Sometimes they bound together ten or more men in a circle around a straw or hay stack, then set fire to the stack. The victims dragged each other into the flames; they all burnt alive. Elsewhere, the captives were tortured before execution by walking barefoot over a carpet of glowing embers several metres long. Where the captors had enough time, they tore off all twenty nails of the victims with pliers. The enjoyment of seeing them suffer was enhanced if they went to a nearby smithy to make the tools red hot on the forge. Wherever they were able to find coal, they took the opportunity of roasting the victims alive. When they skinned somebody alive - usually prominent people who had to be punished prominently, a well-to-do burgomaster, lawyer or physician -, even some of the partisan women were on the verge of fainting, as numerous women also took part in these brutalities.

They were especially cruel to priests and monks. In most cases, they stripped them naked and cut a strap in the shape of a cross from their backs. Then, for the sake of the toughest partisan women, they started to deal with their genitals, tearing their testicles with pliers, cutting off the penis. If there was a forge nearby, they burnt the penis of clergymen with red hot iron, repeating the torture for several days. Modern sawmills also gave ideas for new methods of killing.

Mutilation of the hands or feet with large circular saws was an example of murder with long and excruciating pain. Once the guiltless owner of the sawmill stayed home with all of his family. The troop, punishing without formal sentence, bound all the family to the sawing-bench, and started the machine that cut the man, the woman and the children into two.

Here we should stop to rest after enumerating these horrors, but we must mention another method of killing, the medieval or even older tradition of impalement. The last recorded instance of impalement took place in 1907 in Rumania. That is how Rumanian royal law punished the leaders of the peasant's uprising. Serbia was the only place that still had some "experts" in the art even in 1944. These experts were impaling executioners who preserved the "tradition" of the form of execution causing the greatest possible suffering, as described below:

A pale more than three meters long must be peeled smooth. It must have an iron tip and it should be made slippery with grease. The victim is laid flat on his belly and his torturers step on his shoulders and his bottom so that he would not be able to move. They put a loop on both of his ankles and the two executioner's assistants pull his legs in opposite directions. The chief executioner cuts the trousers on the thighs with his sharp knife, not sparing live flesh. Then he fits the tip of the pale covered with iron into the anus, paying attention to set it in a way that the pale goes along the spine, not touching the heart, so that the victim will suffer long enough. Then he takes a club and hammers the pale in the marked direction, while his aids pull the body onto the pale by the ankles. The tip of the pale should come out behind the clavicle. At this moment, they put the paled man into the formerly dug ditch and it is the triumph of the executioner and the delighted audience if the man groans on the pale for several hours...

HISTORICAL ANTECEDENTS

The Hungarians occupied the Carpathian basin at the end of the 9th century. At that time, the territory of the present Vojvodina was settled sparsely by Bulgarians, but they soon merged with the Hungarian population. The immigration of Serbians started in the 15th century. As a consequence of the more and more threatening attacks of the Turks, the Hungarian king Sigismund signed a contract in 1426 with Istvan Lazarevic, the Serbian vojvode, declaring the Serb his vassal. The southern Hungarian population started to move northward, fleeing from Turkish attacks, and fleeing Serbians took this territory. In a mere four years, between 1479 and 1483, more than 200 thousand Serbians were transferred to Hungary. Numerous Serbians fought against the Turks in the Hungarian army.

The Turks occupied the central part of Hungary in 1541 and they were chased out in 1686 by the United European Forces, under Prince Eugene of Savoy. It was then that a mass immigration of Serbians to Hungary started from Serbia, which was still under Ottoman rule, after the suppressed revolt against the Turks in Kosovo in 1690, the Christian nations on the Balkan peninsula were encouraged by the Austrian Emperor Leopold. Serbian patriarch Arsenije Carnojevic from Kosovo Polje, sought asylum in Hungary with his people consisting of 36 thousand families. At the time, the Serbian newcomers were not considered permanent settlers, only temporary guests.

A letter written by Emperor Leopold to the patriarch testifies to this; "We will strive with all our force and all our ability to lead the Serbian nation that fled to our country back to their former land and to expel the enemy from there, with our victorious arms and with the help of God."

However, this did not happen. Serbia remained under Turkish rule for a long time. A century the Serbs who were granted asylum in Southern Hungary came up in 1790 with a claim of territorial autonomy. In 1848, after the outbreak of the Hungarian War of Independence, they attacked the Hungarian army in the rear and proclaimed the Southern part of Hungary an independent Voivodina.

They did this in spite of Law 1848,XX. of the Hungarian Parliament which ensured complete ecclesiastical and educational self-government and free use of their native language to the Serbs, something for which a parallel could not easily be found in relation to the rights of any other nationality in Europe at the time.

After the suppression of the Hungarian war of independence by the combined forces of Austria and Russia, Voivodina was governed directly from Vienna for a short time, but it was reannexed to Hungary in 1860.

At the outbreak of World War I, the Pan-Serbian movement, encouraged and fully supported by Russia, openly declared that their aim was to destroy the Austro-Hungarian Monarchy and to unite all the Southern Slavic nations living on its territory under Serbian rule. All over the world, Southern Slav emigrees started propaganda activities. Together with the Czech emigrees, led by Masaryk and Benes, they undertook the production of an unbridled level of propaganda rare in modern history. In a memorandum given to the English and French governments in May 1915, they referred to Bácska and Bánát (also to Croatia and even to the south-western part of Hungary) as "Yugoslav national territories" under the name of Vojvodina. They tried to justify this by the false statement: "On this territory, our nation lives in a compact mass and almost without merging with other races". In order to understand the real situation, we must turn to the data of the 1911 census referring to Bácska, when the Serb population was relatively the highest, the proportion of the Hungarian population was 40.5%, the German population 29.7%, Serbs and Croats together did not reach 20%.

Although theoretically the Trianon Treaty ending the war referred to the lofty Wilsonian principle of the "nation's rights to self-determination", what happened in reality was exactly the opposite. Two-thirds of the territory of Hungary was annexed to the neighbouring "victorious" states, along with three and a half million Hungarian inhabitants, who were not asked to whom they wanted to belong. On the annexed territories, systematic liquidation of the Hungarian national minority that lived in a unified block started immediately. For instance, **Princip**, a half-official newspaper in Voivodina wrote the following on September 22, 1922:

"The eradication of the Hungarian race is the foremost task of the Slavs awakened after the war. In the course of a few decades, the tiny Hungarian oasis must be occupied with a systematic and aggressive Slav imperialist policy. Hungary must vanish from the map of Europe. The fate of minorities should not be a problem for Europe, because Europe can be consolidated only by the strengthening of national majorities, thus it is her duty to assimilate minorities."

These principles were also put forward in practice by the Serbs. In schools, they forced Hungarian children with various tricks to go to Serbian classes; they put an end to the training of Hungarian teachers; and they transferred a lot of Hungarian teachers to Southern Serbia, where there are no Hungarians. During the agricultural reforms, the Hungarian and German minorities were banned by decree from the right of claiming land. Hungarian minorities who remained without a living were encouraged to emigrate. In the first two years, around 27 thousand Hungarian emigrants left their birthplace. In place of the expelled Hungarians, the new Yugoslav state settled more than 15 thousand families of civil servants and many thousands of "dobrovoljac" settlers among or next to the remaining Hungarians.

Fortunately, the harassment of national minorities in Yugoslavia subsided after a few years and more peaceful years followed for the native Hungarians. As a result, Hungarian statesmen, in agreement with the Yugoslavs, showed a readiness to forget all the injustices of the past for the sake of appeasement. The two countries made a contract of eternal friendship in this spirit on December 12, 1940.

On March 25, 1941, Yugoslavia joined the German-Italian-Japanese Tripartite Treaty. However, on March 27, a government crisis broke out in Belgrade, and the new government was not willing to ratify the agreement signed with the axis powers. A few hours after receiving the news, Hitler decided to sweep Yugoslavia out of the way of the planned campaign against the Soviet Union. He demanded the military aid of Hungary for this action. Pál Teleki, the Hungarian Prime Minister, firmly opposed Hitler's demand. He could not reconcile his honour to attack a country with whom he had signed a treaty of friendship. However, on April 2, German troops crossed the border of Hungary and started military operations against Yugoslavia. Hungarian officials of foreign affairs were afraid that if they continued to resist the German demand, Germany would occupy Hungary too. They also reasoned that Yugoslavia, as the state with which Hungary had a treaty, had ceased to exist. Thus, they decided to reoccupy the historic Hungarian territory annexed to Yugoslavia. Prime Minister Pál Teleki shot himself at the dawn of April 3, under the weight of moral responsibility.

On receiving the news of Pál Teleki's suicide, Winston Churchill sent a message to the Hungarian nation in the name of Britain and her allies to the effect that, in memory of the great Hungarian statesman who had refused to violate a treaty, the

15

victorious powers would leave a chair empty in the course of future peace talks. Churchill and his victorious allies forgot all about this promise; Churchill does not even mention it in his memoirs. At the peace talks, only the accusations of the enemy were listened to; the much graver atrocities committed against the Hungarians remained unheard.

On April 11, 1941, the Hungarian troops crossed the Yugoslav-Hungarian border and reoccupied the territory of the former Bácska in a few days without much resistance, as the Yugoslav regular army had been forced to withdraw by the military operations of the German army. After that, they still had to take into account the guerilla actions of the still royalist Serbian chetnik organisations. These actions started as soon as the reoccupation began. For example, in Zombor, the Chetniks left 40-50 youths hiding in attics, who started to shoot at the soldiers after dark, who were walking around the town unsuspectingly. The Hungarian soldiers who were not used to ambushes started to shoot at random in sudden panic. Walking in the streets remained very unsafe for Hungarian soldiers garrisoned in some mostly Serbian towns in Vojvodina, as they would always risk becoming targets for snipers. In these circumstances, the number of partisans killed after the Hungarian occupation can be considered very low. According to Yugoslavian data (Zlocim okupatore u Vojvodini, Novi Sad, 1946), the total number of deaths during the Hungarian occupation was 2142 persons. The majority of these people died in armed resistance during guerilla fights, others, mostly Serbian chetniks, and numerous Hungarian communists, were executed after summary justice.

The local population was hostile towards the Serbs settled in 1918 in order to transform the ethnic situation by force, and supported their resettlement to their original dwelling place, Southern Serbia. In their place, 13,200 Hungarians (Székelys) from Rumania (Bukovina) were settled in 1941.

The Yugoslav Communist Party soon organized acts of sabotage and terror. In the "Lenin-letter" published at the beginning of July 1942, they described in detail how to carry out arson, poison the livestock, blow up railways, etc. As a consequence, the court of the Hungarian general staff condemned 93 people to death at summary courts within one and a half months for sabotage, arson and murderous attacks resulting in 56 deaths. 64 of those condemned were executed, but those who participated only in the organization and did not actually commit a crime, got away with a few years of imprisonment.

In spite of the sentences of summary courts, the organized

activities of Serbian partisans continued in the Southern parts of Vojvodina; this fact worried the Hungarian authorities. Tension was increased by the fact that numerous criminals joined the ranks of the Hungarian national guard under the pretext of pursuing the chetnik gangs. These criminals were seeking illicit profits in the chaotic situation and they kept even the Hungarian population in constant fear. On January 12, 1942, the Hungarian military staff reported to the Minister of the Interior that the partisans had concentrated their forces in Novi Sad and that a raid was necessary. On January 21, they put up notices in the streets of Novi Sad, announcing a general raid. On the first day, around 25 to 30 chetniks were shot to death. Lieutenant-General Ferenc Feketehalmi-Czeydner, the leader of the raid, found the level of Hungarian retaliation insufficient. On the news of such strict proceedings, chief of staff Ferenc Szombathelyi ordered that the atrocities cease immediately; they did not cease for another two days. Members of the national guard went from house to house demanding documents, arresting suspicious individuals; then shooting them by the Danube. Besides partisans, probably several hundred innocent people lost their lives.

The news of these atrocities soon reached Budapest, where Endre Bajcsy-Zsilinszky, member of Parliament, demanded the strictest criminal procedure against military leaders who had acted irresponsibly. The chief of staff set up a special committee to investigate the affair, and after a temporary interruption, Regent Miklós Horthy ordered the completion of the legal process. While clearing up the precedents, the investigation concluded that during the summer of 1941, acts of sabotage and fatal terrorist attacks had become more and more frequent, which proved the existence of wide-spread communist partisan activity. In January 1942, there were many fights with Serbian partisan troops. The Serbian population supported the partisans. As a consequence of this situation, the military leaders were in such a peculiar psychological state that they judged the situation much graver than it actually was, as a result of the rumors of the civilian population. They ordered heavy retaliation based on unverified information; they left individual instances of excess unpunished; and even encouraged them. In the confusion that followed, unjustified massacres were not rare. The gravest incident happened in Novi Sad between January 21-23, 1942, when they massacred the Serbian and Jewish population at random, killing 879 people altogether. A total number of 3309 civilians, including 147 minors and 299 elder men and women died in Voivodina (including the victims of the Novi Sad massacre). On the basis of these facts, the prosecutor demanded the meting out the hardest punishment on the officers who were completely mindless of their inhumanity and their duty. However, before the declaration of the sentence, the officers escaped to Germany with German help. The verdict was finally passed in 1946, and then the sentence in some cases was heavier than justified.

The events in Novi Sad were heavily exaggerated by Serbian propaganda. However, **the Serbian vendetta which followed two and a half years afterwards and which was ten times greater in size and many times graver in cruelty, was completely hushed up.** Moreover, it was a taboo subject in Hungary over the last four decades, because the prestige of the Tito-regime (the Tito-myth) could not be destroyed, and because the other "socialist" countries would have been alarmed since they had treated the Hungarians in more or less the same way at the end of 1944.

COLD DAYS - A NOVEL AND A FILM

Author: When my novel "Cold Days" and later in the film based on the novel appeared, I was reproached for the fact that I had discussed only the injustices committed by Hungarians without even mentioning the ten times greater Serbian vendetta, something nobody else had mentioned either.

Interviewer; What was your aim when you revealed in 1960 things that had happened during three days in January 1942 in Novi Sad?

A: among others, I wanted to tell everything that was committed in the confusion of war, against innocent Serbian and Jewish people, at the command of a few blood-thirsty officers, unworthy of the Hungarian nation.

I: Did you have another intention besides naming the delinquents, as if taking the responsibility upon yourself instead of the innocent Hungarian nation?

A: Yes. I hoped that there would be a Serbian writer who would reveal in response the cruel series of massacres that paranoid, sadistic Serbians committed against tens of thousands of innocent Hungarians in Voivodina in the autumn of 1944.

I: Were your hopes fulfilled in the form of Serbian writers making the same symbolic act of collective regret, if not a confession for their crimes like the one you had made in **Cold Days** ?

A: None of my hopes were fulfilled. A few Serbian writers voiced their opinion that in World War II almost two million people lost their lives in their country, so these few tens of thousands of Hungarians should not be of interest to them, especially not as writers.

I.: Did not the memory of these forty thousand Hungarians weigh upon your soul?

A.: Of course it did! The cries addressed to me have put more and more of a burden on my conscience, making me understand, although too late, that I should have presented the Serbian vendetta at the same time as the executions and murders committed by Hungarians. However, this was not possible at the time.

I.: How did you react to the indifference of the Yugoslav writers?

A.: The only thing I could do was to make myself a promise; as soon as it is possible to cry out laud about the cruel weeks of those blood-curdling events, the massacre of innocent Hungarians in Vojvodina in 1944, I will do my best. That is why I have written this book.

Budapest, April 1992

19

Vendetta. Retaliation Multiplied:

WAS THE MASS-MURDER COMMAND ISSUED?

In October 1944 the Hungarian Army abandoned Bácska (Vojvodina) and shortly after the Red Army, under the command of Marshal Malinovsky, crossed the Tisza river. Following the Russians and under their protection, Tito's partisans, the so-called People's Liberation Army, took over the defenseless territory.

The Serbian troops arrived under very strict order in Bácska; they had to "show the strongest possible determination against fifth columnists, especially against Germans and Hungarians".

The term "fifth column" is applied to the subversive and resistant forces and organizations left behind by a retreating "enemy".

The National Committee for People's Liberation and the Red Army had agreed on the necessary cooperation in due time. The partisans were well aware of their bloody task.

About the establishment of the military government, Josip Broz Tito said the following; "The liberation of Bácska, Bánát and Baranya requires the quickest possible return to normal life and the establishment of the people's democratic power in these territories. The extraordinary conditions under which these territories had to live during the occupation, and the necessity that we overcome all the misfortunes of our people caused by the occupying forces and foreign ethnic groups requires that, in the beginning, the army concentrate all power in order to mobilize the economy and carry on the war of liberation more successfully."

Brigadier General Ivan Rukovina was appointed commander of the military administration. He was in constant and direct contact with Tito, the supreme commander. In his first decree, he ordered his troops to "protect the national future and the Southern Slavic character of the territories". This sentence was meant to encourage the alteration of the existing ethnic proportions, in today's terms, **ethnic cleansing.**

In the Oct. 28, 1944 issue of **"Slobodna Vojvodina"**, the newspaper of the People's Liberation Front in Voivodina, one member of the Regional Committee of the Yugoslavian Communist Party summarized the intentions suggested from above, which were to be planted into the heads of the fierce partisans; "Although we destroyed the occupying German and

Hungarian hordes and drove them back to the west, we have not yet eradicated the roots of the poisonous weeds planted by them... The hundred thousands of foreigners who were settled on the territories where our ancestors had cleared the forests; drained the swamps; and created the conditions necessary for civilized life. These foreigners still kept shooting at our soldiers and the Soviet soldiers from the dark. They do everything they can to prevent the return to normal life, preparing, in the midst of this difficult situation, to stab us in the back again at the appropriate moment... **The people feel that determined, energetic steps are needed to ensure the Yugoslavian character of Bácska."**

The title of the article, **"Historic Decision"**, clearly demonstrates that it contains not an individual's brain-child but the guiding principles of the higher leadership unashamed of falsifying history as well as the present. The historical falsification is that it presents the Serbs as the ancient inhabitants of the area who were deprived of their lands by intruding foreign ethnic groups over the centuries. The contemporary falsification is that one of the allegedly intruding nations, the Hungarians, kept shooting at the partisans from the dark; which is nothing else than the tactics typical of the Serbian snipers called chetniks (later the communist partisans) employed against Hungarian soldiers during the reoccupation of Bácska.

In reality, the Hungarians living in Bácska, although lots of weapons were laying around the fields after the front passed through, did not fire a single bullet either at the Russian soldiers marching through or at the Serbian partisans who came into power.

The vengeance on the Hungarians, the idea of the vendetta, was implanted deeply in the minds of the partisan commissars who were in constant touch with their commander, General Rukovina. Rukovina in turn had to inform Marshal Tito about all his decisions and all the "military" achievements of his subordinates. In short, it is impossible that Tito, the supreme commander, was not informed at least once a week on how the purge or rather the slaughter of the "fascist" Hungarians was going forward.

The Yugoslavian government, as soon as it got in touch with the new temporary democratic Hungarian government, declared its demand for an exchange of population. They offered forty thousand Hungarians living in Bácska for the same number of Southern Slavs who were to move there in their place. This demand, however, soon became obsolete not only because the Serbs and Croats who remained in Hungary did not wish to move to Tito's Yugoslavia but also because the Yugoslav authorities were well aware of the fact that the forty thousand Hungarians they offered had already been "resettled" in the next world.

Jovan Veselinov Zharko, secretary of the Regional Committee of the Communist Party, said the following, on April 5, 1945; "We have changed our position towards the Hungarians, we must improve their awareness of the fact, that they live in this country and should fight for it."

This intention, however, was very hard to fulfil. First of all, the horrible weeks of vengeance had to be covered over with a veil of deep silence and forgetfulness.

In his book entitled **"The Birth of the Autonomous Voivodina"**, Veselinov Zharko tries to draw a sharp distinction between himself and the murderous deeds that took place outside his secret scope of authority in the autumn of 1944 in Bácska; **"Certain chauvinist groups began to emerge, which cried for vengeance on the whole Hungarian population.** Due to them, serious mistakes and excesses took place, which certainly had their consequences. Instead of calling the real accomplices of the occupying forces to account, those who participated in their numerous crimes, in some villages they punished certain ethnic Hungarian civilians who had nothing to do with the bestial crimes of the fascists.

Certain persons coming from Yugoslavian headquarters along with other uninvited guests sneaking into Bácska also caused us some trouble. This applies especially to the National Defence Department (**OZNA; Odeljenie za zastitu naroda**), whose members for a while possessed the authority to arrest anybody without any obligation to inform the political leadership of the territory where they were operating..."

The OZNA later became infamous under the name **UDB** (**Uprava drzhavnie bezbednosti; State Security Authorities**).

Of course, with such opinions Jovan Veselinov Zharko could not remain the head of the Regional Committee in Novi Sad for very long.

The murder commands were issued and carried out without his participation. Later he said the following; *"You must understand, everything that happened in those days was inseparable from the Party. There was never any question about that."*

PEOPLE OF BEZDÁN

1.

On a May afternoon, while I was dedicating copies of my newly published book for interested readers in front of a major theatre in Budapest, a man in rural clothes approached me after having gazed at me for a long time. He held a seemingly brand new copy of "**Cold Days**" in his hand and, answering my inquiring glance, he quietly said;

"Are the Bezdan people in it?"

I did not reach for his copy, the simply dressed man obviously did not want my signature, he was only interested in the fate of the people of Bezdan. I knew that news of their fate had not reached my book.

I was sitting in front of the theatre, a couple of metres away from the traffic, sheltered from the hot sun by a tent. The bookseller girls had already mentioned that somebody from Bezdan had been looking for me in the morning, but they had no idea where Bezdan was. So this curious question, whispered in a low voice, did not take me by surprise.

"Should they be in it?"

"Of course they should," answered the Bezdan man, "because it belongs to it, we must not forget that."

"Why do you think such a thin book should contain Bezdan?"

"For the things that happened there."

I could have asked what of importance happened there, but instead, I was curious of the date, when. I knew that the recollection of a date, of an exact day and hour is the weakest point; not only of most simple men, but of most educated men as well; if one wants to prove the incorrectness of an assertion. The Bezdan man was not embarrassed by this unexpected question, the date was on the tip of his tongue as it must have been in his mind during the previous twenty years;

"November the third, nineteen hundred and forty four, from morning till late afternoon."

There were more and more people gathering around us with books in their hands. I asked him twice to tell me about that event twenty years before, but my man could not say more than:

"The soccer field...", and again, "the soccer field..."

I had to realize that he was not willing to say anything more in front of strangers, so I decided that once I was done with those who wanted my signature, I would take him to a nearby restaurant to try to loosen his tongue.

Some minutes later I was already reading the menu, offering several good meals for lunch but he said he was not hungry and accepted nothing more than a glass of red wine. Then I reminded him of the third of November for the third time.

"My only luck was that I had left for Baja on horseback on the evening of November the second," began the man at last, "because my brother-in-law had sent word that my sister Julis might give birth to her child any hour and he was still in service, and he didn't know if he could stay with her. My mother didn't dare go, my father couldn't, because he was a deserter from the army and he spent most of his time in the attic behind the chimney. My little brother was not yet over sixteen, so he was too small to help our expectant sister. So the duty, and the luck, fell on me."

"Well, it must have been quite dangerous to ride on horseback in those days", I said sympathetically.

"I was not stopped by anyone on the way, although even the ditches were full of refugees, especially near the crossings where the traffic was very heavy."

"How can you remember the events of that day then, if you had to go to Baja?"

"My mother preserved each hour of that day and the previous evening in her memory and she passed it on to me."

He fell silent, this time I did not say anything to encourage him, I just filled his glass.

"My mother said that hardly had I left, when at dusk, the armed partisans began to cross the Danube on barges. She also heard some shots but no cries; they must have shot into the air. Early in the morning, the village drummer announced that everybody, for his own good, must gather on the soccer field. Under penalty of death, no one was allowed to remain at home, not even the sick. My father also climbed down from behind the chimney, he thought that the crime of desertion was over anyway, since the death penalty announced by the Hungarians on deserters was no longer in force. He decided not to go back to the attic; he washed and shaved, and obeying the order, walked to the soccer field together with my mother and my little brother. A gramophone was playing there. It played Serbian partisan marches, but sometimes they put on the record *"You are so beautiful Hungary"* and *"I am a soldier of Horthy Miklós",* perhaps as an encouragement. The partisans, who had machine guns, were not more than twenty, a partisan woman was the loudest among them. With the help of interpreters, they ordered that the men between sixteen and fifty to remain on the soccer field and the rest, elderly people, women, children, leave the village and go to the farms. No one was allowed to go home, until they had gotten permission. Shoving them with their guns, the partisans began to drive the people in the direction of the farms. The women started to cry at that point, they were worried because the people had been divided into two groups. Fear fell on those who left, but also on those who remained on the field.

My brother, who was not yet sixteen, and my father, who was well over fifty and belonged only to the army reserve, wanted to join the majority, but the more they protested the stronger they were pushed back among the group of men staying on the field. The partisan woman I mentioned before, hit them brutally with her rifle butt. There were one hundred and eighteen men chosen to die, but the partisans couldn't agree how to kill them. First they drove them to the bank of the Danube, where some of them were shot into the river by machine guns. My father and my brother were among these. Maybe they didn't find the current of the water strong enough, since some of the bodies were caught by some hidden whirlpools. Therefore, after some quarrel and debate, they began to drive the rest towards Zombor.

In Zombor they didn't get anything to eat for weeks, every day dozens of people starved to death were pulled from the barracks. Those people who were forbidden to return to the village dispersed in the countryside in the nearby farms.

My mother got back to the battered house only after more than a week, left utterly alone. While hiding, she had thought of walking over to our Julis in Baja, who gave birth to a healthy boy the next week. My mother didn't want to leave because she was worried about the livestock in the stable and the sties; she was the only one there to feed them. After several days, she returned to find the cow was gone; somebody had driven her away. Perhaps it was fortunate too, otherwise it would have perished in front of the empty manger. The pigs were gone too, just a couple of frightened hens came forward at my mother's call.

Those who had hidden at home and hadn't gone out to the soccer field had met their fate according to the threat. Some bodies were found in the wells; others had to be dug out of the dungheap, only their arms or legs stuck out of the muck as if they were trying to ask for help; "I am here, help me."

"What happened after that ?"

"Nothing. After my mother had come back from the farm no one harmed her. Later it was even announced that they should report if they were molested or if anything was missing from the house. Everybody knew that they had found all the stables and the pantries looted and my mother had nobody to accuse of stealing the cow and the pigs. Those who had come to the village by barge on the second of November were by that time replaced by others. The murderers simply disappeared.

A man called Bosnyak who lived in Bezdan and had been a lieutenant in the Yugoslavian army seemed to know some of them and tried to protest. He went up to the commander of the gunmen, already on the bank of the Danube, and tried to explain in Serbian that they must not do that, they could easily get their fingers burnt for it later, since these people were all innocent and faithful citizens of the future Yugoslavian state. At this, the partisans began to beat the former lieutenant, screaming that nobody could talk about faithfulness here; nobody was innocent here but they were all murderers and traitors and the whole village should be exterminated without trace. This lieutenant called Bosnyak was executed among the very first people together with my father.

"Wasn't there any further resistance?"

"No, nothing. Although there were not more than twenty of them facing several hundred, they had an awful lot of weapons, guns and hand grenades hung on them everywhere. That's what I don't understand till this very day. There were still a lot of rifles and hand grenades lying around in the houses, which had been brought home or left behind by deserters once they had changed clothes. The Bezdan people who had hidden all this military equipment never thought of taking these weapons out to defend themselves against the partisans. They were planning instead that the grenades would serve well for river fishing and the rifles for hunting once the world quieted down again.

"Do you demand revenge for the things that happened to the Bezdan people?"

"Oh no! I wouldn't even know who to take revenge on. I am not sure if anyone could find the people who committed these murders. I can only think of my little brother, who couldn't be guilty at his age, and my father, who also wasn't guilty of anything, my mother swore upon that.

"Then what do you want, what do you expect?", I asked in a low voice. In response, his voice rose sharply.

"What do I want? I want everybody to know, we were innocent! We were all innocent! I want somebody to announce that those people all fell victim to murder innocently."

"Nothing more? Don´t you want to search for the murderers, to catch them?"

"The murderers can't be found anyway, they have hidden and those who could have remembered, who could have testified were all killed by them. I have never heard and never read about anybody who knows how many people perished in each place, because people are afraid to talk; they are all frightened even to remember those days. The authorities in Bacska strictly forbid anybody to recall it and those who try to speak about these events are arrested. We are allowed to remember and to speak only about what happened in Novi Sad." At this point he put his hand on my book, "and you can write only about that, too, although..."

"Yes, you´re right, "I admitted. "Even here in our country we are allowed to remember only those crimes we committed or which were committed in our name in January 1942. According to the Hungarian government, the rest should be forgotten since, it was considered just retaliation and therefore not mentioned even at the peace negotiations."

"But it was not just because lots of innocent people were slaughtered!"

My Bezdan man drank up his wine with one gulp and grew extremely agitated.

"This silence which was ordered on us afflicts us Hungarians the most! Can you imagine anybody who can forget everything that is good about his own people and everything that is evil about other nationsí Anybody who is willing to remember his crimes only and forgets all good deeds, all excuses but regards the enemy as pure, innocent and faultless almost to the extent of glorification. Even if he remembers an evil deed he declares it an inevitable, brave, heroic act, although he is well aware that such bloodshed is far from being brave heroism."

I was surprised and became suspicious that he was aiming at accusing me for my book. All I said, however, was that I felt the danger and the absurdity of the orders requiring silence, but I hoped that there would be a brave Serbian writer, who would write the story of the deeds the Serb partisans committed in the name of his nation in Bacska during the autumn of 1944.

After a brief period of thought, the man said the following:

"No Serb will ever confess to what happened in Bezdán and in Bácska."

"So you want a kind of revenge after all!"

"No! Not revenge! There´s no one to revenge and no one to take revenge on. I will not go to court nor will I take up arms. I just feel sorrow for my little brother who died in the river without knowing a man's life at all. Had I known beforehand what would happen to him, I would rather have gone with my father and sent him away to our sister in Baja."

"Is that all?"

"And don't forget to mention that the other one hundred and sixteen people were all innocent as well."

I decided to satisfy his wish and, as a first step, to make public what I had learned from him about the vengeance of the partisans and about the innocent people of Bezdan. I asked him where I could find him if I wanted to know something more about that autumn.

"It's better not to find me, or if they happened to learn that it was me who gave the information and broke the order of silence, I could go home no more and if I tried, they would kill me."

We bade farewell with a strong handshake. Although he had learned in front of the tent that a dedication is a "gift" of honour from the writer to the reader, he did not wish to obtain it even after our conversation. Only later did I understand that he was afraid of telling me his name. He felt that even this could be dangerous for him.

I put down the story of my meeting with the Man of Bezdan on the same day. A couple of days later, I told the audience of the University Theatre all I knew about the murder of the 118 people. My audience was shocked by this unknown tragedy.

I hoped that I could publish the account of this experience soon after the appearance of "**Cold Days**". Unfortunately, only years later could I find a periodical, **"Kortárs"** which dared to publish the story the **Man of Bezdan** told me. Our mutual boldness was followed by an international diplomatic conflict, **Tito's impending visit to Budapest was postponed because of us and the association of Yugoslav partisans declared me persona non grata**. That was the reaction to breaking the obligatory silence.

2.

Dr. András Varga, an engineer by profession and head of the department at the University of Heidelberg, came to Germany from Bácska. Fortunately, he does not have to worry about the vengeful retaliation and, as a "foreigner", he was able to gather a lot of information about the events of that horrible autumn including the massacre in Bezdan. He also managed to identify the bloodthirsty and murderous Serbian partisan squad. He shared his knowledge and the results of his research with Miklós Zelei, who published the still dangerous historical data in the Sept. 15, 1990 issue of the weekly "**Képes 7**".

According to the Hungarian professor, the Hungarian armed forces, the police and the gendarmerie abandoned the city of Subotica (Szabadka) in northern Bácska on Oct. 8, 1944, and the Soviet troops marched in from the direction of Szeged on Oct. 14. They reached Zombor on Oct. 20, and Novi Sad two days later, on Oct. 22. The Serbian troops, the partisan squads of Tito, infiltrated Bácska only after the fight ended in the region.

The report pays special attention to Bezdán, this Hungarian village on the left bank of the Danube. To the best of Dr. Varga's knowledge, the villagers, men, women and children alike, were summoned to the soccer field at 9 a.m. on Nov. 3, 1944, under the pretext that important public works should be carried out and therefore everybody must show up under penalty of death. The partisans separated all 18 and 19 year-old young men from the crowd, including the players of the well-known soccer team, the BFC. By this cynical move, the partisan commander wanted to mislead the remaining population and make it possible to drive the group away without disturbance.

Equipped with spades and hoes, 122 men were led along the road to Zombor to the edge of the Isterbac woods. Armed with machine guns, only 15 partisans escorted the obedient and slightly worried group. Once there, they were forced to dig two large, wide pits, each 2 meters deep. At that point, some of them may have begun to suspect the purpose of the work. Their apprehension could have been reinforced by the fact that a kind-hearted partisan tried to send back a 13 year-old boy to the soccer field who came with the group, holding his father's hand. The little boy proved to be very affectionate; he could not be separated from his father. Their "job" being urgent, the partisans no longer cared for him. They forced the men to pile their spades and hoes and shot first the soccer team, then the rest of the group together with the child into the pits. It seems that no one thought of taking up his spade and fighting against the handful of gunmen. After the last man had been executed, they sent a messenger on horseback to the soccer field with the message that "the job is done". On receiving the news, the partisans who had so far guarded the unsuspecting crowd let the new widows and orphans go home.

After a few days, a division of Bulgarian soldiers arrived in

Bezdan. The report does not reveal whether the partisans had left by that time to continue their bestial operations in other villages. The Bulgarian commander was told of the events of Nov. 3. He gave permission to open the common grave and give the dead a proper burial. The funeral into separate graves took place on Nov. 28. The opening of the grave revealed that the victims were tied with wire in groups of fifteen. It is amazing that people whose hands were still free did not revolt against their murderers on seeing this; even the last group stretched their hands obediently to be tied with the rusty wire. Another forty corpses, mutilated beyond recognition, were found in the cellar of the village council house and in nearby yards, twenty more in the water of the Ferenc Canal. These were buried at the same time as the bodies from the two big common graves. Thirty-two bodies could not be identified due to the horrible mutilations; these were reburied in one common grave.

Dr. Varga found out the name of the murder squad. **The horrible crimes were committed by the 12th Udarna Brigade of the 51st Partisan Division, under the orders of the commander and the political officer (commissar).**

3.

To begin, I am attempting to give a factual account of the bloody autumn of one single village, but the mercilessly enforced silence had different effects on different memories. Those who dare to speak are still frightened by the threat of revenge, because no Hungarian in Yugoslavia is allowed to speak about that autumn of 1944 when the Serb partisans returned. They are afraid even to tell their children what they preserved in their memories about those brutal days of slaughter.

It is not easy, perhaps not even possible to understand how hundreds of thousands of people can be forced into silence by the ice-cold, remorseless terror for almost half a century. Although we are not able to lift the ban of silence ordered by the state (perhaps secretly enacted under penalty of death), yet we may perhaps be able to reconstruct the events of the past from several uncertain memories.

I managed to get hold of certain parts of the memoirs of Gy.L. from Bezdan, which were written in 1944. F.R., T.K. and Gy. M. told me their memories in 1974. None of them, however, wishes his name to appear here. Those who lived through the era of fear can never forget the shadow of danger. Life is really cheap in the past and present Serbia.

"Saturday, October 21, 1944. At 11 P.M.. the Hungarian army and the gendarmerie abandoned the village. Some people say that the Russians have already taken Zombor. "I am watching the street from the corner of the window", Gy.L. writes.

October 22. At dawn I saw some armed men on the other side near Marci Dóka's house, there were about twenty or twenty-five of them; they were Royalist chetniks. They had been hiding in the Korcza woods and came out when the front arrived. In the morning they went to the council house, hoisted the Yugoslavian flag and appointed the new village principals.

October 30. We dug a pit at the end of the garden and hid our best cutlery, clothes and bedding in it. Like others, we also had to take the radio and the bicycle to the council house. Besides the chetniks, one or two Russian soldiers could be seen on the streets. The people, visited the church and the cemetery. The tension of the first days have slowly subsided.

November 2. In the morning a row of horse drawn wagons arrived from Zombor. When the first wagon stopped at the council house, the last in the line reached back further than the Stein house. After the wagons, the soldiers of the Twelfth Brigade came. The headquarters was established in the Drimóczi restaurant. In the evening we heard shots. After ten or fifteen minutes of gunfire, the partisans occupied the council house. People say the communist partisans have killed all the Royalist chetniks .

November 3. There are a lot of Russian soldiers and partisans on the streets. Trucks full of weapons and ammunition are coming along the main road. The Russians have turned the house of lumber-merchant Kiss into a slaughterhouse. They occupied the restaurants and the schools and moved field hospitals in some big houses.

Around 9 a.m., I was in front of Pali Frank's house when I saw five or six partisans going into a house on the other side. I suspected something dangerous, so I quickened my steps to get away before they came out. They took the young men away to forced labor. I noticed with surprise that none of them had any tools.

The town crier announced on every street corner that everybody must gather on the soccer field at 1 P.M., because the commander of the Twelfth Brigade was giving a speech.

It was gloomy, overcast and light rain was drizzling. There

were big puddles on the soccer field. We stopped at a drier place far from the grandstand. We were surrounded by soldiers; there was a partisan with a machine gun at every fifteen or twenty steps.

The tension was unbearable; it was obvious that they wanted to massacre all the villagers. Seven thousand of us were waiting for the moment, holding our breathe, when the machine guns would open fire.

I couldn't see what happened on the stand, I just saw three Russian officers coming on horseback. Those who stood near the stand later told me that the partisans wanted to kill us all . János Juszt, who was the vice chairman of the people's committee at the council house, knelt down and begged the commander to have mercy on the village. Some people heard as the Russian officers cursed and told the partisans, "There was enough bloodshed, let these people go home!"

We were ordered from the stand that everyone must leave the village by 6 P.M.. and go at least six kilometers away. Women and children were allowed to go, but the men between eighteen and forty had to remain.

I have never seen such a mess as followed that order. Everybody ran like hell, but the soldiers chased them back to the field. There was only one free road towards the engine-house, but there was a deep ditch there full of water and you could cross it over a little wooden bridge three or four steps wide. The whole crowd was pushing that way, crying, screaming, yelling, shoving and treading on one another as if some lunatics had been let loose from a madhouse. Two armed partisans stood on guard on each side of the bridge and chased back each man who wanted to cross the ditch. When I was whirled onto the bridge by the crowd, I walked almost crouching so that even my hat couldn't be seen. I was drifting with the throng and we got past the bridge at last. Everyone ran towards the embankment and then home.

In the afternoon we also left for the farm of my brother-in-law. From the corner we saw that the men who had remained on the soccer field were escorted in columns four abreast towards Zombor. The road was full of refugees. There were wagons loaded with bedding, others were pushing wheelbarrows, almost breaking their backs in the effort. It was very difficult to get ahead, since the road was flooded by all kinds of military vehicles, tanks, trucks, batteries pulled by horses."

The recollections of F.R.:

"It was announced by the town crier that everyone must come

to the soccer field. They want to find nobody at home, except the ill or the elderly people unable to walk.

Then on the soccer field they surrounded us with machine guns. The whole village stood there, awaiting their fate. In the meantime, the Russians were working on the telephone line by the Danube and their commander saw the big crowd and the machine guns all around. He asked the soldiers:

"What's happening here?"

One of them answered:

"Our commander wants to give a speech."

"Where your headquarters are?"

"The third building from here; that big house over there."

The Russian jumped on his horse and came back with the partisan commander within ten minutes. All we saw was that when he got to the place where the machine guns were, he took out his blackjack and bang! He beat the partisans within inches of their life. He said:

"Go home, everybody!"

Then the partisans, to hide their shame, ordered that all men under forty must stay there for work. They gathered some five hundred of them and began to drive them toward Zombor in rows of four. When we got to the Kozora woods, one of the partisans shouted:

"Three steps to right and left and load guns".

You know, there was the forest stretching four kilometers long in front of us. My friend András told me:

"Don't worry, this one in front of me can shoot only one."

For there was a partisan marching in front of Andras. After we left the woods, we realized that it was they that were afraid of us.

"Shoulder arms and step back to the group!

Well, we got to Zombor. They counted us; six were missing. Of course, Miska Pázmány, **Joca** Hordósi and those who had a farm near Kozora sneaked away in the dark for it was pouring rain, thunder and lightning. They suddenly lay down and when the group left, away to the farms!

Then we were taken into the military barracks next to the railway. More than five hundred of us from Bezdan, packed into three rooms. They gave us nothing to eat for four days. A partisan woman came in each day and beat us with her rifle butt. They wanted somebody to strike back and then they'd'have had a reason to execute us all.

In the first days of December, they began to let us go home. Fifty people left on December 6. Our turn came the next day. Toncsi Tomasics, Gyuszi Horváth and Törő were not set free;

they held them there as hostages.

November 4, right after dawn, I got up and went out to the yard. I drew a bucketful of water from the well and, half naked, I washed myself. It was prickly cold outside, but I didn't feel it at all and the cold water drove sleep out of my eyes.

I was just towelling myself, when I heard sobbing coming from the yard. I quickly put on my shirt and ran to the entrance door to ask what happened? Someone said that Pista Libis had been shot dead.

"By who and where?"

"By the partisans at Isterbác where he was led yesterday after 1 o'clock."

Pista Libis was coming to the soccer field yesterday with his wife when two partisans stopped him and carried him away.

It seems that the worst I feared has come true. The partisans massacred the men at Isterbác. They drove them there to execute them, not to work. It is too horrible to think about; one hundred and twenty-one innocent people were murdered!"

The recollections of F. R.:

"My nephew, Lajos Kiss, was also visited by two partisans.

"Get dressed; you come with us to work!"

His two children ran out of the house and hugged both legs of Lajos. One of the partisans asked him in Hungarian:

"Are these your children?"

"Yes, mine."

"God damn it!", he said. "Go inside, you can stay here!"

An hour later two other partisans came, and these two took him away. Poor guy, he didn't think about hiding somewhere. So he was taken away and he was the third to be shot.

Jani was set free for he had been a lieutenant in the Yugoslavian army, but he demanded that the others must be set free as well. When this partisan woman called Julka started to shoot, Jani flung himself at her and almost twisted the machine gun out of her hands. The partisans then got very frightened and started to shoot at anybody in sight. Jani got twenty bullets; the woman got none. He was the first man who died at Isterbác.

The father-in-law of Toni Limburger was the last. When the partisans came in, the commander asked Toni:

"Is it you whose house was smeared with shit by the Germans because you didnát join the SS?"

"Yes."

They gave him an ID.
"You can come and go freely. Do you have anybody at Isterbác?"
"Yes, my father-in-law was taken away."
"Then, he said, get your bike and follow me!"
They rushed off, the partisans on horseback and he on bike. But when they got there, some hundred meters away from the meadow, it seemed to smoulder, the dead bodies lay there in rows. All the partisan said was:
"Antal, we're too late, let's turn back."
So Toni was the first to know that everyone had been shot dead at Isterbác."

The recollections of T.K.:

"Jani Bosnyák, when he heard that the partisans had taken some people out to Isterbác, put on his Serbian reserve officer's uniform and hurried after them. He got there when the first ten men were led up from the cellar. He spoke perfect Serbian and he asked Julka to set these people free, because they were innocent and never did any harm to the Serbs. Julka told him to go home, but he stepped among the others voluntarily and he was the first to be shot dead."

The recollections of Gy.M.:

"The partisans went from house to house and said that the bridge at Kigyósi had been blown up and they had to repair it, but the people were taken to Isterbác, not there. The nicest house in Isterbác was that of the Major's. They were locked up in the cellar of that house and the partisans brought them up in groups of ten. They had an old gramophone with handcrank and they played partisan marches. My brother-in-law, Pista Magyar, was also there. One of his eyes had been plucked out when very young, so he looked kind of miserable. They told him to go away but never look back.
"Well, he said later, I couldn't run more than a hundred steps when I heard: bang, bang, bang! The folks of Isterbác were watching it from the attics; the gramophone was playing; they were drinking brandy from bottles; and Julka and two men mowed people down with machine guns."

35

The recollections of F.R.:

"Rudi Nyárai came home from Budapest where he was working as a weaver. His father was also a weaver in Bezdán. They were shot down together, embracing each other. Jóska Braun, died at Isterbác; he was a cripple. He married a Jewish girl and worked as a furrier. He was also taken away when he said that his wife was a Jew.

"No, you are just another Swabian!"

He didn't die right away, he crawled on to a straw-stack and cried for help. The partisans had already left, but no one dared to go there and so he bled to death."

November 5, Sunday. The Russian army is moving toward Bezdán on the main road just half a mile from us, car after car; wagon after wagon; batteries of artillery, tanks, trucks full of soldiers. The advance started yesterday. It seems that the Russian army wants to cross the Danube at Bezdán.

Old Libis came back from Isterbác. He buried his son temporarily at the site of the execution. The rest of them still lay there unburied; the relatives don't dare to go there since they are afraid that they themselves would be shot. He told us that there lay teacher Csépe, Pista Amrein, Péter Láng, János Láng, Imre Balla, János Horváth, János Kiss, Imre Kiss, József Mari, József Sipos, János Pócz, Sándor Turi, István Midlinszky with his two sons, János Győrfi, György Kisbéri, Pali Major, János Mazák, Józsi Szántó, Feri Varga, Jani Kedves, Feri Jankovics.

In the evening, we all came together in the big room of the farmhouse, lit some candles and prayed for them until late at night."

The recollections of T.K.:

"The mother of Jani Bosnyák was the first who dared to go out to Isterbác. She pulled Jani, her son-in-law, and her grandson out from under the dead bodies. She laid them side by side, threw some earth on them, then brought twigs from the forest and made a temporary cross on the graves. She came to the farms crying and wailing. Her pain must have been unbearable; the Virgin Mary couldn't have suffered more than her."

"*November 24.* After a two-week long battle, the Russian army managed to cross the Danube. Troops are moving along the road from dawn to dusk, but the more people cross the river, the more arrive from Zombor, Gy.L. writes.

December 6. While the inhabitants were away on the farms, the Serbian folks from Monostor came to plunder with wagons. They took away everything, bedding, furniture, valuables.

There were some people who, in spite of the orders, hadn't left for the farms, because they didn't want to leave their houses unattended. Uncle Pista Kedves stayed at home as well. When the partisans found him, they beat him up with rifle butts so brutally that he passed out several times. Then they locked him up in the cellar of Sándor Horváth, but that cellar was full of people. Every morning they were driven out but each time he was pushed back.

"You are stary (old), you can go back!"

The young people were executed in the yard (all he heard were the shots), later they were found buried in the dunghill.

December 8. There was a mass again in the church. Chaplain Lajos Vajda, who had been taken to Zombor on November 3, by the partisans, returned. He was given food and accommodation at the Győrfis'. The women were cleaning the church for days. They carried out several loads of garbage and dung, because the soldiers had put themselves up in the church and kept their horses there too. They had even made a fire in the middle of the church; the place where it was can still be seen.

December 10. Life slowly starts again, people gather and bring news. There is no village in Bácska where the partisans didn't take a deadly toll. They executed twenty-eight of the Catholic priests, among them the abbot of Becse, who was beaten to death, and Bálint Dupp, the parish priest of Csurog, who was executed in Becse. In Topolya they threw the hundreds of corpses into the lake behind the council house. In Temerin, Péterréve and Bajmok, they made the victims dig their own graves. In Novi Sad they shot thousands of Hungarians dead on the soccer field. In the villages near the Tisza river, they shot them into the water. The Swabians of Bácska were taken to the camp of Gakovo, which was surrounded with barbed wire. They slept there in the open and were kept there until they starved to death. I also heard about men who were buried alive, impaled or quartered. In Zombor they buried their victims into the ground up to their necks and then crushed them with tanks."

The recollections of T.K.:

"The executions in the villages of Bácska were directed by a woman called Julka. She made a bloodbath wherever the 12th Brigade went. This Julka said that each executed Serbian must be avenged with the death of ten Hungarians. She kept mentioning seven thousand executed Serbs, so she wanted the death of seventy thousand Hungarians. She died at the Battle of Batina when they crossed the Danube. A shell tore her hand off and then she was taken to Bezdán for first aid. Ilus, whose husband was also executed at Isterbác, worked at the first-aid station and saw her die. On the hill of Batina, it is her statue on the top of the thirty-yard high granite monument. It can be seen on the side of the column how they crossed the Danube."

The recollections of F.R.:

"I was looking for Laci, my brother-in-law, and I was going around everywhere in the village. We picked up seven dead bodies in the big mill; seven at Miklós Stein' on the main street, five in the Knipp-school; five at Miska Flesz'. There were also seven corpses at Pista Szécsényi's house on Puszta Street. Then another two, one, three   were dug in yards and dunghill or thrown into wells.

There was a long ditch along New Street. The partisans told the people: if you run away, you can escape. Poor fellows, they were wired to one another. Instead of running together, they tugged one another right and left till they all were shot into the ditch from behind; there were seven of them.

At Uncle Józsi Tallósi's, the well was dug on the corridor. They drew the water from there and poured it right into the kitchen. In April he wanted to put the pub in order and open it. He tried to draw some water but couldn't. They opened the well; it was covered with planks. They found it full of dead bodies almost up to the top. When he reported it, he was told:

"They can't be taken out; fill it up."

Then there was one, I can't understand that, who was dug into the ground, and his head was crushed totally flat. I saw another who was slashed open from neck downwards and his heart was cut out. We found him like that when we dug him out.

December 16. I met the forester of Topolya in Zombor. In Topolya they executed people on the hillside at dusk. They made them dig their graves, undress to underpants, and then shot them into the pit. Early next morning, when he found the place, the earth that had been thrown on them was still moving. They spoke of about 1,600 executed people in Zombor.

March 12, 1945. The relatives of the executed asked the Serb leaders several times to let them bury the dead, but they were refused. "Let the dogs carry their bones away", answered the commander each time. They were only allowed to throw a little earth on the bodies; legs and hands stuck out here and there. It turned warmer and the stench of the decomposing corpses at Isterbác grew more unbearable every day. After the intercession of the Bulgarian troops, the Serb leaders at last consented to their proper burial in the cemetery.

"May God give them eternal rest and us peaceful hearts to live in this country without anger and hate", as our fathers and grandfathers did. The earth of Isterbác has soaked up the blood of the victims.

4.

Having examined the history of the parishes in Bácska and searched the country clergymen's consciences, Márton Szücs, retired parson of Bácsszőlős, and József Kovács, retired parson of Martonos, wrote **"The Silence Of The Dead"**, a comprehensive work, which serves as a requiem for the 40,000 innocent Hungarian victims in Bácska.

Though registering war crimes is considered a bold courageous step in itself; living in Bácska, they did not dare publish the book during their lifetime. The requiem could only be made public by other daring men after the death of the authors.

In October and November 1944, wrote the courageous parsons, a murderous thunderstorm blew in on the gentle plains of Bácska, and demanded at least 40,000 Hungarian victims. The overwhelming majority of them were innocent and were killed without a just cause in bloody revenge. Those who were guilty of assaulting the Serbs between 1941-44 had fled in time, thus the cruel vengeance came upon completely innocent people at home. Some Serb politicians and Yugoslav pseudo-historians claim that the massacred Hungarians were all fascists, and therefore war criminals. However, this statement lacks any basis and is completely false. This work attempts to reveal the innocence of 99% of the Hungarian victims. It also points out the fact that legal proceedings should have been taken against the guilty, as was done in Hungary following the atrocities in Novi Sad and its surroundings. The authors protest against the probable accusations, that this account was written to incite revenge; this would make no sense at all. Its sole purpose is to demonstrate that the overwhelming majority of the massacred were innocent, guiltless of any wrong deeds deserving retaliation.

The minority Serbs in the village of Bezdán did not have to endure any persecution or discrimination in 1941-42.

At the end of October, Russian troops marched into the village. A few days later, on November 3, partisans followed the Russians. At about nine in the morning, the villagers, men, women, children alike, were summoned to a general meeting on the soccer-field. 122 men were picked out from the crowd and ordered to bring a spade or a hoe with them. The partisans drove these 122 men under armed guard to a farm near the Isterbác woods. They locked most of the men up in barns, and forced some to dig pits. On the farm a kind-hearted partisan guard asked the housewife, "Do you have any relatives in the barn?" She answered, "My nephew is there." The guard kindly shook his head, saying, "Unfortunately there is no back door in the barn. I would have let him out, but I cannot."

When the digging men finished working, the guards sent away the residents of the farm, saying, "Leave for an hour; we have some work to do here." Then the partisans led the men in the barn to the edge of the pits, and fired rounds of bullets at the unsuspecting victims.

There was a 13 year-old boy among the slaughtered; the son of the poundmaster. The partisans wanted to separate him from his father, but the affectionate child did not want to leave him.

The ferocious, bloodthirsty partisan heading the executions was a woman called Boyka. Upon seeing the child, who was so strongly attached to his father, she told the soldiers, "Kill the kid too! You have to strike at the root of the evil!" Then she had the boy killed.

Boyka took her accordion out and started to sing triumphant marching songs at the unburied corpses of the innocent Hungarians. Having done that, she sent a dispatch rider on a white horse to the partisans on the soccer field, with the message "Gotovo ye!", which means "Done!".

The partisans on the soccer field sent the parson with the women and the children to the farms, and escorted the remaining 500 men and the two chaplains to the Kronich Palace in Zombor. All this occurred at around two in the afternoon.

Later on, the partisans were relieved by Bulgarian soldiers. The Bulgarian commander allowed the exhumation of the slaughtered men. The common grave was opened on March 28th. It was discovered that the victims had been tied together in groups of 15 while marching toward the pits. They had been murdered at the edge of the common grave, with their hands roped together.

Previously, on November 18, the villagers had found other corpses in the cellar of the parish hall and in the streets, mutilated beyond recognition. There were 20 more corpses in the Ferenc Canal.

György Prolich had been forced to get off his wagon in the outskirts, and was executed then and there.

In order to save his father, József Schmidt had said that if his father was released, he would reveal the place in the woods where the enemy's radio transmitter was hidden. All this had been invented by him just to play for time. As the partisans could not find a trace of the transmitter, they tortured and finally executed the dreadfully mutilated Schmidt.

While the executions were going on in the vacated village, the Serbs of Monostorszeg continued to plunder Bezdán and rob the unattended houses. It is possible that these Serbs were the murderers of the elderly who stayed at home, disregarding the order of the partisans proclamation.

In the winter of 1944-45, the executed were registered in the death roll of the Roman Catholic Parsonage in Bezdán, pp.242-254. There was a slight hint that the local Serbs were not to be blamed for massacring the 183 innocent victims, but rather the partisan commanders, and foremost the partisan woman called Boyka.

This is the list of the executed men from Bezdán, in order of registration and age:

Ferenc Csapó, 33	Mihály Miovács, 18
Sándor Ferenc, 35	Sándor Zezula, 20
János Kanizsay, 16	József Midlinszki, 19
István Midlinszki, 40	Imre Szkerlesz, 38
János Kedves, 46	Ferenc Varga, 33
Sándor Molnár, 37	Péter Lang, 28
Károly Macskál, 52	István Kiss, 18
János Bosnyák, 35	György Oberreiter, 19
Péter Kalmár, 29	János Virág, 28
Kálmán Szakács, 30	János Kiss, 30
Mihály Hettyei, 25	József Nagy, 42
Mihály Knoll, 37	János Balla, 44
József Limberger, 48	István Kartalis, 45

József Csapó, 23
János Kiss, 32
Ferenc Csapó, Jr., 19
Ádám Stein, 45
János Pócz,
István Bálint, 32
Imre Sipos, 40
József Hummel, 26
József Fitza, 42
Ferenc Szingler, 31
Pál Kubik, 45
Imre Balla, 37
Sándor Lovász, 30
József Plesz, 17
János Kiss, 43
István Szarka, 18
Bálint Hódosy, 20
János Győrffy, 43
Gyula Kelsek, 16
János Horváth, 44
József Braun, 38
Antal Nagy, 21
Mihály Sziklika, 20
József Hettyei, 20
János Spolarits, 52
M. Baron, 52
Antal Elmer, 24
Gyula Kőszeghy, 27
István Libis, 35
József Szántó, 40
Ferenc Bodrogvári, 39
Ferenc Kidlinszki, 18
Izsó Szabó, 44
Lajos Kiss, 31
Imre Kiss, 20
László Varga, 25

János Brettréger, 29
Ferenc Mári, 39
István Stein, 51
Jenő Csépes, 37
József Pampulik,18
János Kiss, Jr., 17
János Kazák, 18
József Schmidt, Jr.,22
Mihály Flesz, 53
István Anrein, 45
Szinon Takács, 24
László Fatay, 30
István Magyar, 21
György Kisbéri, 20
János Németh, 17
Rudolf Hummel, 48
József Magyar, 43
István Zsámboki, 37
Jakab Braun, 53
János Nagy, 22
Sándor Kedves, 43
Ferenc Mári, Jr., 13
János Neveda, 19
Simon Szekszindler, 18
János Leiffer, 53
Sándor Veiner, 45
József K. Sipos, 17
György Kovács, 51
György Lengyel, 49
Pál Mafer, 33
László Koller, 22
Géza Kleer, ?
Gyula Zarubeszki, 48
Imre Szabó, 44
Unknown
Ferenc Flesz, 54

The summary reveals that this death roll does not include all the victims who were found and exhumed. The unidentified corpses were buried in the common graves without their data having been recorded.

The 102 Catholic victims can be distributed according to their age into the following groups: 25 under 20, 24 between 21-30, 22 between 31-40, 19 between 41-50, and 3 with unknown ages.

According to the victims' occupation, there were 10 students, 2 civil servants, 1 teacher, 7 tradesmen, 11 craftsmen, 10 workers, 17 farmers, 12 hired men, 5 inn-keepers, 2 sailors, 1 horse-dealer, 1 poundmaster (also called dog-catcher), and three unknown who were murdered.

The roll displays that a man called Bosnyák, wearing the Yugoslav first lieutenants' uniform, was christened János, and was only 35 when he died in the fire of partisan machine guns. The man from Bezdán, coming up to me at the book stall in front of the theater in Budapest, might be Ferenc Flesz's son, consequently, his younger brother, József Flesz, 17, can also be found on the roll. The poundmaster, to whom the small child clung so strongly, was registered as Ferenc Mari in the death roll.

Yugoslav politicians and state security forces were all for concealing, suppressing, or nipping in the bud all kinds of testimony and the collection of data concerning these events. When there was any trace of such intention detected, the authorities retaliated immediately.

We must be thankful to the two well-remembered parsons, who were passing from village to village, collecting data in deep secrecy under cover of church service.

Since there are several memorial writings concerning the antecedents of the massacre in Bezdán, namely, how the men were gathered and abducted, the data remain unsure to some extent. I was also uncertain regarding the details of these days, and especially those of November 3. However, the following is certain: the Hungarian troops retreated from Bezdan in mid-October, and only 30-40 gendarmes remained in the village for a few more days. When they were informed, however, that the Russians had already reached Zombor, they set off at once on Saturday, October 21.

On Sunday, poorly armed, Royalist chetniks arrived in the village together with others who were thought to be Serbs from Monostorszeg. Frightening the villagers by firing their guns in the air , this rabble were looting eagerly; stealing money and jewels; changing their shabby clothes to tidy ones; though wearing their hats to preserve a soldierly look.

Having heard about the advance of the Red Army, they left immediately. The Russian troops arrived by horse-drawn or powered vehicles and tanks, and occupied Bezdán without fight or funfair on October 29.

On All Saints Day, the 12th Partisan Brigade arrived at Bezdán.

They put themselves up at Drinóczi and Hermann Inns. However, they only began to carry out their plans on Friday, November 3.

"About two weeks have passed since the retreating German troops crossed the Danube and reached the western shore. Large and small partisan troops kept coming to our village. A week ago, three Russian scouts arrived on horses and provided safe conduct documents to the Hungarian soldiers, if they wanted to return home. We were happy to see that the Russians were so kind.(N.B. The Soviet Army behaved well in Yugoslav teritory, because it was a "liberated allied country". In "enemy" Hungary it was a totally different behavior). Compared to the situation during the German retreat, the village seemed a place for rest and peace. The front line Russians insulted or hurt no one. Three or four days ago, some two hundred Russian soldiers arrived by horse drawn carriages. The village council ordered the people to provide as much food for the soldiers as possible, since the supplies of the troops were inadequate; the villagers fulfilled the request.

On November 3, at seven in the morning a partisan came to our house, informing me and my sister's husband that we were to leave for forced labor. We asked him what tools to bring with us. He replied that no tool was needed, since we will find everything there. On leaving, we saw the partisans collecting people, going from house to house. Each of our groups was escorted by 20-30 of them as we set off toward the Isterbác farms (2-3 km. from our village).

Our group was led to the fenced-in yard of a large farm, where there had already been some people loafing around, waiting. We did not feel closely watched at all. At ten o'clock the situation changed. Partisans armed with machine-guns surrounded the people, who were supposed to have been gathered to work, and lined them up in the yard. The culling began. Construction laborers and hired men were ordered to step out of the line. Then the partisans gave them a short speech and led them off. Before all this, the native German speaking men, and those from Szállás had been collected. I suppose the partisans just intended to pick out the members of the Szálasi Party, (Hungarian Quisling Party, which supported Hitler's policies and formed, -with the help of the German Army- the last war government October 15, 1944, after the second armed occupation of Hungary.(farms were called "szállás"), they collected 15-20 men poor tenant-farmers and smallholders. Then the craftsmen, tradesmen, and the educated had to stand forth. Those few still standing in the line were asked whether they had any relatives serving in the German or Hungarian armies, and how much land or property they possessed. Those having several houses or land holding larger than 20 acres, or those wearing middle class-like clothes were to join the group standing forth. The few of us remaining in the line were escorted to the garden outside this yard, and were given the same speech as they gave the construction laborers. Then the partisans released us. Those remaining at the farm were led to a locked building, and later massacred at the ditch behind the farm in groups of ten.

While we were in Isterbác, the partisans at home announced at around eight in the morning that every villager, even the bedridden should appear on the soccer-field by noon, as they would go from door to door and shoot all the people found at home then and there. The partisans' intention was to massacre the people on the soccer-field, but it failed when a partisan officer appeared on a white horse and spoke to their commander. We had seen this mounted officer in Isterbác, before being released. Thus the situation on the soccer-field changed completely. The men age 16-60 were gathered, and some 5-6,000 villagers were led to Zombor, where the partisans locked them up in a building. For three days these people had to stay there with guns pointed at them all the time. Meanwhile they received neither food nor drink and were not allowed to meet their bodily demands.

The women, children, and the elderly remaining at home were compelled to leave the village in two hours. Meanwhile several executions took place. At that time, I was hiding in a hayloft at a farm together with others 13 kilometers away from the village.

A month passed before the circumstances grew safer, then the local headquarters requested the villagers to appear. We were collected and told to volunteer to join the Petőfi Brigade. 99% of us refused, so we were compelled to enter labor service. I was taken to Zombor, then Sztapár, and in January to Monostorszeg, from where we escaped on May 8, 1945.

Please do not publish my name, as I sometimes return home even now, and there may be some people who would hurt me with pleasure. What I have written down can be verified by the elderly of our village."

"On this Friday morning Páter Láng, resident of Bezdan, was busy in his yard chopping wood or sweeping when the partisans passed by, leading his friends.

"What are you up to?", he asked cheerfully.

"A bit of exercise!", they answered in jest.

"Good for you", Peter said, waving his hand.

Then the partisans brought him out of the yard and included him in the march leaving for Isterbác.

His name is on the death roll. Age 28."

Hungarian sappers guarded the mined bridge of the canal. They were ordered to blow up the bridge upon retreating. However, what the sappers only longed for was to change into civilian clothes and stay there. They were fed-up with the already lost war.

The arriving Loyalist chetniks were thought to be the final authority by the Hungarian sappers, therefore they offered a compromise: If they were given safe conduct papers, they would not blow up the bridge, and would hand over their guns. The chetniks agreed to the offer. After the capitulation, they massacred all the sappers on the spot next to the unexploded bridge.

"On November 3, I got up at five in the morning. As I went from the cottage to the spare room, I heard our small door slamming. So did my father, who was rubbing down the horses in the barn, where there were two cows as well.

Before the reoccupation of the village, he had already received his draft-card from the Hungarian Army. Then he and my mother had decided that he would be hiding in our farm in the Sziget, where no one would find him. He had taken two calves with him.

On November 2, 1944, it was growing dark when my father returned with the two calves. In the evening, when we went to bed, he said that the war was over for us, and soon we would be happy again. In the morning he spoke to me for the last time, saying, "Pray for me, son." It was the first Friday of the month and I observed a novena (a Catholic Friday prayer service). Right after high mass, partisans surrounded us with grenades in their belts, levelling their machine guns at us. The men, also observing a novena, were separated immediately and dragged off to Isterbác. It is true that everyone who observes First Friday will not die without being absolved. I do not know the exact number of the victims, but I am sure that they had all received the Holy Communion. By the time I got home, the partisans had already taken away my father. He was to unearth tanks that hindered the partisans' advance. My mother asked them whether a shovel was needed, but they answered that everything that was needed could be found there.

In the morning, the town crier was walking around in the village, reading aloud an announcement, which said that all the people able to move should be on the soccer field by noon, and those found at home would be shot dead. At about two in the afternoon, the partisans began driving the villagers together with machine guns. At around three they tolled the church-bells and started the massacre. My father may have been one of the first victims. In the evening we had to leave our home, and father had not returned.

Mother hitched the horses to the wagon on which we had loaded food and clothes. We were about to leave for our farm, when two Russian soldiers entered our yard and unharnessed the horses. We could hardly make them understand that we were badly in need of horses. Then they brought two pony-like ones, but mother had to adjust the harness, as it did not fit these small horses. We set off for the farm with mother and my father's mother, practically pushing the carriage and the two exhausted horses; we arrived late.

There was already a rumor going about, that the gathered people were all killed at 3 o'clock in the afternoon. The victims were told that, in the event that they should resist, the whole village gathered on the soccer field would be massacred. They were tortured from morning to 3 o'clock, first in a cellar then in a shed. A record player was on, while the partisan woman sitting on a horse watched the people being driven into the water in groups of ten. Those dressed well were forced to strip, so some of them had only their underwear on when they died. My father was ordered to take off his brogue, winter coat, and watch.

Mother went to look for father, but in vain. During the executions, a German plane was taking photos, and this allowed three men to escape across the river.

When mother returned with the news that she had been unable to find my father, we still hoped that he would appear, since there was a forest next to the river, and the farm behind it with 3 acres of land, that belonged to mother. We were hiding in the farm, when we saw soldiers approaching. After a while a mounted militia-man came looking for mother; he told her that father had been one of the massacred victims, and the place they had left him. Mother and some of our relatives went there and buried my father, but they could dig just one spade deep since the ground was already frozen.

The Militia man said that the corpses of two boys from Hercegszántó, workers of the Hangya (Coop General Store), and other corpses were covered with water and could not have been buried. The militia dug a common grave and laid 24 dead bodies there. A militia man told the others to check on the river once again. They entered the murky river hand in hand. One of them bumped into something, then all of them went there and found another corpse. They could not pull it to the shore, so they brought two or four horses (I do not know exactly) from the farm in Isterbác, and harnessed them. The horses dragged the dead man out of the water with a chain hooked to the neck of his coat. The militia- men laid him into the grave as the 25th victim; he was my father.

My mother's married sister was hiding a 20 year-old man, Sanyi Zezula, in her loft. Looking for men, the partisans entered her house too. My aunt said, "My husband is here!" They replied, "He is too old; isn't there a younger man here?" My aunt answered, "My son is hiding in the loft." "That's who we want! Ask him to come down!" He was shot dead.

The two grandmothers lifted a door off the hinges; laid his body on it; wheeled him home on a Wheelbarrow; and laid him on a bed. When the partisans came, they expelled the grandmothers from the house and found the dead boy in the bed. Since they thought that he had been a partisan, they wanted to massacre the village in revenge. However, a militia-man soothed them explaining that the boy was a Hungarian and had been killed in Isterbác. Therefore, both grandmothers and all of us were saved."

The new occupying army was Bulgarian. We asked them to help rebury the dead in the cemetery. On March 25, 1945, the exhumation began. At the entrance of the village, there was a limebarrel with shoe disinfectant in it. No one was allowed to enter or leave the village. Graves were dug in three rows in the cemetery; the hearses came one after the other with two coffins on each; and the kinsmen followed the carriages. Those in the fore of the march had already reached the cemetery, when we left from home.

In my father's inside pocket, we found a photo of my sister and me, soaked with his blood, except for a small part covered by a 10-pengő bill; I still have this photo. In the cemetery two partisans caught my mother and me and threw us into the cellar of the parish hall. Our vicar was looking for us, and told the partisans that he would not bury the dead until we were released; so they set us free. The vicar was my grandfather's schoolmate.

When we entered our house we found 60 Angora rabbits, 40 sheep, 2 cows, 2 calves, some 100 hens, geese, and ducks in one room. Someone stole the sow, and the piglets, and the shop was robbed (My father was a tradesman.).

Mother and my younger brother had to work at the hemp factory, a part of which had belonged to our family. Every 24 hours, I was compelled to look after the injured partisans at the infirmary; I was escorted by armed partisans; I felt horrible.

The vicar would come every night. He would knock on the door with his stick and beg mother, "Rózsika, run away with the children! They want to kill you!" So one night we crossed the Hungarian border at Hercegszántó on a Bulgarian truck. We got off at a ditch, and at dawn we started to the police station to register. It was awful! We had to move heaven and earth just in order to gain enough money so we could afford to move to Baja."

"My name is Marta Anna Margin; my younger sister is Maria Barbara; my younger brother is Robert. My mother's name was Mrs. Istvan Margin born Rozika Horn. My father, István Margin was killed at the age of 45."

Gyula Zarubszky from Bácska, having converted all his property into cash in Budapest, returned to his hometown Zombor in 1941. He rented and ran the local Elefant Inn till the fall of 1944. He never cared for politics too much; he and his family just lived in the town as true Hungarians. In our childhood, we his kinsmen from Budapest spent the summers there. In 1944 we stayed in Zombor till August.

Mother told them to move to Budapest, but uncle Gyula waited to departe from home until October. He came by a hore drawn carriage with his wife and mother-in-law, but they were stopped at the bridge and had to turn back because the Germans were using it for their retreat. They stayed at a peasant cottage in Bezdán, and waited for permission to cross the river. Then the partisans arrived at the village, and a few days later announced that every man should report to them. My uncle was wearing only a shirt when they carried him off. At the gathering place, according to my aunt's account, the partisans separated the craftsmen. The rest were led to a cellar. My uncle engraved his last words into the wall of the cellar, "Gyula Zarubszky from Zombor, they will execute me!" He was 35. We have never learned the exact reason for his death. We can only suppose that Tito's partisans wanted to murder all Hungarian men.

My aunt returned to Zombor, and kept looking for her husband. A few months later, a common grave was opened, and she could identify her husband's corpse among the dead with the help of his dentist. A tombstone with his name on it stands to his memory in the cemetery of Bezdan.

In the summer of 1945, my aunt and her elderly mother received permission to return to Hungary, leaving all they had behind."

During these weeks, the Red Army occupied Bezdan until early

December. They left for Baranya across a pontoon bridge, which had replaced the bridge blown up by German rear guards. Earlier, they had tried several times to build the pontoon bridge while bombing Batina Hill, but they were hindered by the heavy fire of the German and Hungarian artillery from the other side of the river.

The villagers, expelled to the farms, were allowed to return a few days later. By that time the revenging partisans had left for other villages to obey their commanders' bloodthirsty orders.

The death roll compiled by priests and parsons contains the names of the 183 victims found in Bezdán. Those who died in Zombor are not included. According to some who still remember, the fall of 1944 demanded 350 victims in Bezdán.

UJVIDÉK, RENAMED NOVI SAD

"On October 23, 1944, Todor Gavrilovic Rilc, Political Commissar of the Partisan Division in Novi Sad, flew the red-starred flag of the new Yugoslavia from the tower of the Hungarian built Ujvidék City Hall.

During the day, the 7th Vojvodina Brigade marched into Ujvidék, Capitol of the Province. The Serbians, old and young of the town, crowded in the streets welcoming the liberating partisans. Flags, red and in national colors, with five-pointed stars, were fluttering everywhere. Slogans resounded cheering the party and Comrade Josip Broz Tito. The Hungarians stayed indoors.

The enthusiastic and happy citizens mingled with the soldiers and together they celebrated", remembers Jovan Veselinov Zharko, the newly appointed Municipal Party Secretary, recalling the Serbs' feelings concerning the day when Ujvidek was renamed Novi Sad.

György Szigethy, Hungarian citizen from Novi Sad, has completely different sentiments compared to the Serbs' solemn mood.

"On October 20, 1944, the last gendarmes left Novi Sad, which fell on evil days then. The first Soviet and partisan troops arrived on October 22. During these three days, the town's unofficial leader was a Serbian Orthodox Priest named Olimpia.

Escorted by some partisan officers, a Soviet major came by car; there was great ovation. When a Russian military truck arrived loaded with Russians and partisans, with much difficulty the major got out of the car. The major was lifted onto a platform, with a 5 liter demijohn in his hand. Raising it to his mouth, he drank deeply and made the long-awaited welcoming speech; on the occasion of having occupied the city:

"Well, zdrastvutye!"

There was another great ovation, when a partisan officer presented the regards of Comrade Tito and of his liberating army. Then Olimpia welcomed the liberating brothers.

That night the terror began in Novi Sad."

One of the reasons that the Serbs regarded the shabby-looking partisans as their liberators, because they killed the Hungarian enemies of the Serb hosts for a bottle of spirits.

If Bulgarian troops, marching across the region had arrived on time, a great number of Hungarians could have been saved.

On October 23, the partisans started arresting Hungarian men living in the district west of the railroad line dividing the town. Usually guided by a local Serbian resident, armed partisans with machine guns carried Hungarians off every night. They destroyed Hungarian homes, searching for "fascists" who might be hiding and looting.

Girls and women suffered a lot at that time. The town rabble had its way of pleasing the partisans. Spying on Hungarian houses, they knew where young girls and women could be found. They led drunken partisans to them, and in return they could plunder under the protection of partisan arms.

The captured Germans were collected in the fastener factory, in Most Sumadijska Street. The partisans shot everybody who was reluctant to hand over his valuables.

The Hungarians were led to the former winter port of the Danube. The fort of the former Hungarian river police on Martial Island served as the center for the upcoming massacre. According to the survivors, men were locked up here for days and for months. Some of the captives were 14 or 15 year old boys, "Leventes" (a compulsory apolitical, para-military youth organisation, universally disliked), who were considered "dangerous fascists".

On October 25, a partisan officer appeared in the fort, escorted by a troop of obviously drunken armed men. He read out some 300 names from a sheet of paper by his flashlight. Having finished reading, he put the light in his pocket, waving to his men. They surrounded the selected Hungarians and disappeared in the night with them. After a while, we heard the machine guns rattle and the truck engines roaring.

A friend of mine, who was among the selected ones, had luck. In the summer of 1944 an American bombardment had destroyed the power station near the railroad station, so on the night of the massacre it was very dark. The darkness saved my friend. When his name was read out, he was struck numb with fear. He did not report even at the repeated call, and the officer went on reading as if nothing had happened. His name was not mentioned again. The Hungarians who were carried off from home were massacred according to the roll. My friend had been driven to Martial Island in the morning of October 24. On arriving he saw 4,000 men crowding there. The partisans called out these men in groups of 100, and shot them dead in a quarter of an hour with machine guns. Paralyzed with fear, the captives waited, feeling and knowing that *they must die because they are Hungarians.*

At first the partisans carried off people according to a list of names, under the auspices of the National Defence Department, OZNA (Odeljenie za zastitu naroda). This organ was the forerunner of the dreaded UDB (State Security Authority).

All the victims had stayed in their homeland, because they felt innocent. They had not taken part in the reprisals against the Serb Communist Partisans, therefore, tought they had no reason to flee. As it later developed, their main and only fault was not a particular war crime but being Hungarian.

On the second night, the previous scene was repeated, a roll was read out again. The partisan officer said smiling, those whose names were called may go home. We did not hear the rattle of guns as these men left. Later on, however, we learnt that none of them arrived home.

On the fifth day, the captives on the island received some water and bread.   During the week-end Russian soldiers took some 100 men to work on the reconstruction of the airfield; many of them survived.

During the first week some 1,500 men were killed on the island. Most of them were shot and pushed into the Danube. Some are buried in a land called Shanghai, on the floodplain behind the slaughter house between the highroad to the village of Katy and the Danube. From 1941 to the fall of 1944, this floodplain area had been a frontier zone, where the Hungarian corp of engineers had built a primitive defense line with trenches made from wood and earth. These trenches served as common graves later. Partisans were patrolling railway stations, roads, and trains, and ruthlessly killing everyone who did not have a travel document issued by them.

The partisans murdered the majority of the assembled men. A small numbers of the victims were driven to work but many of them were killed along the way. The partisans shot two Franciscans, Rev. Krizosztom Körösztös, the prior, and brother Kristóf Kovács, and robbed the monastery. Before the Soviet troops marched into the town, Ferenc Svraka, the parson in town, had phoned brother Krizosztom asking for advice, pondering whether to flee or stay. Almost at the same time Tallian, a relative of Krizosztom's, told him, "Brother, the last train is leaving soon. Be ready!"

All this happened before and after the morning mass. Although it was a week day, the flock gathered in such large numbers for the mass, that half of them had to remain outside. At this sight Krizosztom phoned the parson and his relative, the commissioner

of police and said, "I cannot leave
my flock and lose touch with them, as they will need me."
However, he did not forbid his brethren from to escaping but
recommended fleeing. Still, two Franciscans, brother Mihály and
the previously mentioned brother Kristóf stayed with him in the
monastery.

When hunting for Hungarian men, the armed partisans
overlooked the monastery altough a shoemaker working in the
neighborhood warned them that there were men in the monastery.

The partisans told the humpbacked, sickly Krizosztom to stay,
but he refused, "If you do not let my brethren go, take me with
you, too!", he cried and followed the two younger monks.
Krizosztom and Kristóf were slain. Father Mihály survived the
sufferings, and wrote a diary-like report about the bygone events.

"24th October, 1944. Yesterday was Saint John's of Capistrano
Feast Day. In the sky above Ujvidék, the clouds are thinning out,
heading towards Budapest with all the nervousness of the
pursued. Under the clouds geese are migrating to the south
honking dreadfully as if they were saying, "Poor, poor are those
staying here."

We are withdrawing to the monastery. Someone
remarked,"Now only the Serbs and the honest Hungarians stayed
in Novi Sad."

There is some frightened, hidden self-justification in this remark
against a future accusation.   "Why would Tito's partisans
hurt those who have done only good? I know everyone thinks
that all Hungarian are guilty; To be a Hungarian is a deadly sin."

25th October, 1944. I am visiting some patients in hospital
today. Our flag has disappeared from the facade, and their flags
are flapping there. A lad passes by me running, with a newspaper
in his hands, **Novi Sad; Novi Sad** is the title of the new paper.
The red ribbon on his cap follows the boy.

The guards are Serbs already. They are eyeing everyone like
predatory sparrow-hawks.

In the evening, we shiver and huddle together with a homely
warmth, trying to ease the silence pressing our chests by telling
the stories of our lives. We are looking back like the dying.

Our prior, Rev. Krizosztom Köröstös was citing Saint John
Chrysostom his patron saint, who spent his hard life in exile...
Nomen est omen! Now Rev. Köröstös thinks that his patron
saint has something in store for him. He is an inspired Hungarian
patriot, who volunteered for his mission in Bácska. He left the

peaceful monastery in Szécsény, where he had been the prior; he joined the Transylvanian Army Corp as a chaplain.

Rev. Kristóf Kovács was born in Jászberény. Saint Christopher, his patron saint holds Little Jesus on his shoulder, while fording a river. He is a good educator and an especially fervent palmist. Reading his own hand many a time he foretold, "I won't live long! That is what my life line shows, and I will die a violent death!"

I am Mihály (Michael), the protege of the dragon-killing archangel, and a devoted Hungarian son of a Swabian family from Almáskamarás. We are all young. We could live much longer, though Rev. Krizosztom has always been sickly, and he is called "the old one" by the flock because his gouty humped appearance.   We confessed to each other. We studied the Pope's blessing, and the authorization of Rodex for extreme cases.

26th October, 1944. Troops have been marching through the town since dawn, as if pursuing those who left earlier for the Danube. In the morning partisans occupied the streets.They hammered on the doors, thumping with the butts of rifles. When the host lingered, the door was burst open. Guns thundered and people swore. The moans were more and more frequent. All men aged 18 and 50 years old were driven away for an account.

Similarly to an overflowing river, the driven mass flooded every street, like cattle being driven towards the slaughterhouse.

It was a silent, mute march. No one believed that it will be just an identity check.

We cannot speak to our Serbian guards. We were trying to explain to them that Rev. Krizosztom should be freed. They may have freed him, but he stayed, because he didn't want to leave without us.

The fear was rushing along our nerves during the march; will it be a bullet in the back of the head? The waters of the Danube in October are already cold, but it won't matter at all...

We were going to Monarica. New ones kept coming till late at night. We were lying down on the bare floor. I pushed my overcoat under the prior's sore waist.

We heard many hots, one by one or in long bursts.

900 men arrived from Temerin with shovels and picks. Will they dig our grave? Everyone thinks of this.

27th October, 1944. Nothing happened all day. We were waiting excitedly. Small groups kept arriving to join us. At around ten at night, some partisans entered the place holding a long list from which they read out some 300 names. Rev. Krizosztom's name was also mentioned. "You can go home and continue your work.

Since it is already late, you cannot leave for home right now, as it is not secure in the streets. You will spend the night in Pavilion #2."

Those whose names were read were still milling around in the pavilion in the morning.

Around noon, Pavilion #2 was not empty yet.

In the evening we were strictly commanded, "Lay down! No one can go to the window!"

The windows were set so low, that we could see out of them even from the floor. Armed men were standing in two rows in front of the pavilion. A military band started playing.

Some of us sitting close to the windows reported on every phase of the events. "The gate of the pavilion is opening. The captives are coming out tied together in threes. The soldiers are beating them with rifle butts. The prisoners are stopping short. They are trembling. Those who get a harder blow, fall on their knees, and are floored."

Then they were driven away. Later the music drowned out the thundering of machine guns.

29th October, 1944, the old Franciscan priest is said to have been badly beaten! He was beaten to death.

Others report that he had been skinned before being killed, because he had settled Székelys, i.e. Magyars of eastern Transylvania to "Dobrovoljac" (settlers from other Serbian provinces) houses. The latter is true, but we cannot believe that he had really been flayed. In those days, such a long torturing procedure was not used for killing there, as the murderers did not have either the time or the patience for this. What seems possible is that Rev. Krizosztom's piety and his fragile, sickly look, and the fact that he denied even a silent collaboration, provoked the accompanying soldiers to slay or shoot him suddenly.

Thatt night they called out several hundred of us again. After a while we could hear the rattle of the automatic weapons.

30th October, 1944, we were making acquaintances with the others in the camp. The troubles or problemes of others made us forget ours; we tried to make others forget. Kristóf is made friends easily, as there was some charm in his character. He was a magnet, attracting others as if he were attracting iron dust.

We can't accept that we have lost Krizosztom, though he accepted his fate himself.

"I have only one chance to be sacrificed for my Church and Homeland; I cannot let it go." he said at the beginning of the fall.

He took the valuable chalices and sacred cloth of the cloister in Ujvidek to Budapest, and handed them over to the Reverend Provincial. He asked him to stay, because the Serbs were vengeful.

"Coming to Buda was not to save my hide, but save to the valuables of the Order". He refused to accept the possibility of staying in Buda.

In the evening terrible news came, five hundred martyrs were buried in the abandoned trenches.

November 1, 1944, we were crossing the river on a ferry to Fort Pétervárad. Kristóf was hobbling beside me. In his eyes, the rays of the setting sun said farewell. We heard the tolling of the bells from the town. "Kristof! Is it already us for whom the bells toll!"

There was a long wait, then an order came.

"Run! Run!." We have to rush not to be trampled by the guards' horses. Eight hundred captives stopped short at the castle gate, gasping wildly for breath . On the gate there is a big skull and an inscription below, Memento mori!, i.e. Remember death! Why? We could not think of anything else.

The guard beside us asks Kristóf, "What is the time?"

Kristóf tells him the time and smiles, while the guard takes his watch away, saying, "You won't need it any more..."

In the casemates under the fortress, the atmosphere was sepulchral. People kept coming to confess one by one. The officers were taken away.

November 2, 1944. It was said that only two hundred men were to remain here, the rest would be ordered to go farther. We were shrinking back, trying to stay among the remaining.

We heard the fierce shout,

"Papovi napred!", i.e."Priests forward! They are scolding us, we are guilty.

With iron rods, sticks, shovels they beat us. The bones cracked, our faces were bleeding.

They werw beating us till they started to sweat. I was ordered to wipe the others' faces clean. Poor Kristóf had a long cut on the head; he was bleeding heavily. I forget my own wound. We were going forward. The speed of the march was regulated by blows.

Occasionally I cast a furtive look at Kristóf to see how he could keep up with such a wound. We reached a well. Bloody water is running from Kristof's mouth.

In the afternoon he is not able to stand or walk any longer. He has received a hard blow on the leg, maybe one of his tendons is ruptured. Some are willing to carry him, but the guard shouts at us, "Put him beside the haystack!" This was a death-sentence.

"Sic debuit esse", Kristóf said. "This is the way it should happen." "Then shoot me, too", I ask the guard. "Go to hell", he said jerking me after the others.

Then a Russian truck came with a black death's head flag on it. We raised Kristóf onto the truck. I put his cowl on him, too. He was being driven to death.

A young guard addresses me in Hungarian,"Father, why have you stayed here?""Because we love you." He is startled.

"Why should the innocent run away?", I said.

November 3, 1944. The guard who spoke Hungarian warns me while he helped me to a house because, I was about to faint.

"Take off your frock; they will beat every priest to death", he said.   Our host procures a jacket for me from the local priest. My partners were mainly from Temerin. They shared their little food with me.

November 12, 1944. We went to work. Good news came,the aged and the ill can go home. On Sunday morning, when they were leaving, I was hurrying after them but I was stopped by my guard, "You have to stay here." Oh Lord, I am sentenced to death.

A few days pass before we learn that they were not going home, but were shot into the Danube.

I was crushed beneath the burden of God's incomprehensible measures; he wants me to live against my wish.

In 1945 I informed Rome of everything, Father Michael."

Beside shooting the victims into the Danube, some of the corpses were burnt in "Shanghai", next to the slaughter-house.

A German prisoner-of-war, a driver, said in Passau, Germany : "We were transferring men for days from Ujvidék (Neusatz in German); we never carried anyone back. There is a small woods near Szenttamás and Feketics, that is where we were going by truck.

The men we carried there were forced to dig the pit for the mass grave, then they were shot into it. The next bunch of people buried the corpses, then dug their own graves. We buried the last ones, and because we did not have to dig a pit, we hoped that we could drive the trucks back."

In the 1970s a proposed highway was to pass the woods at Feketics, but the authorities rerouted it in another direction after being warned that mass graves were there.

The fate of the Hungarian captives in the fort of the river police who were taken away after the second night call and told to go home, but who never returned was unknown by the remaining prisoners. They did not hear any rifle-fire or rounds from machine guns. These victims were herded to the Guszak quarters, and massacred. Their necks were slashed with knives.

In 1947, those compelled to forced labor were to build embankments on today's Pinki Street, where the embankments in the direction of Guszak had ended. Behind the quarters, the pick and shovel men found a mass grave full of human bones and severed skulls.

The Partisans shot all the captured Hungarian students, too. The students were massacred in the woods of Rajc, after having been driven along the bridge over the canal, close to the slaughter-house, naked and with hands tied together above their heads.

No one returned from the soccer-field of the Cultural Society group in Ujvidék either.

The data, which shows that on the soccer-field alone, ten thousand people were killed, is exaggerated. This number refers to the losses of the whole town.

In the summer of 1941 the Hungarian railroadmen who transferred to Ujvidek officially participated in transporting, and detraining the Csángó-Székelys from Bukovina, (Rumania) and helped them settle at the "Dobrovoljac" place. Upon this score nine unsuspecting Hungarian railroaders, with a station agent and some traffic managers among them, were arrested. As they did not consider themselves guilty, they were not afraid of punishment. However, the partisans, encouraged by the Dobrovoljacs, tied all the Hungarian railroaders with wire to the rails at the station in Piros, and drove the only yard-engine remaining there over them. While the whistle blew once, all of the nine victims were beheaded and dismembered either at the knee or at the shin, according to their height.

SZENTTAMÁS - FÖLDVÁR

Szenttamás has a bloody heritage going back to the War of Independence in 1848-49. Then, openly opposed to the Hungarian government, some troops of Serbian border guards entrenched themselves in the villages which had remains of Roman fortifications. During the year of 1848, the government troops launched an unsuccessful attack three times against these armed Serbs, who were declared rebels.

The first siege on July 14, 1848, was led by lieutenant general Baron Fülöp Berchtold, the commander-in-chief of the government troops. However, the siege began dispiritedly and halfheartedly. Having met the resolute resistance of the rebelling Serbs, Lt-Gen. Berchtold soon gave the order to retreat despite the superiority of the Austro-Hungarians in number.

On the same night, after the siege of Szenttamás, the commander of the Serbs ordered an attack on the neighboring village, Földvár, emboldened by their unexpected success against the Austro-Hungarian forces. The Serbs could march into the town only on the third day of the assault, during which the Serb and Hungarian villagers set each other's houses on fire one by one.

The government troops reoccupied Szenttamás by noon on the 18th of July. In the Catholic church, they found 37 Hungarian children's bodies with the heads cut off. These children must have been the victims of the Serb soldiers.

At this sight the imperial divisions of the army, i.e. the Polish, Czech and German soldiers, who at the time still took the side of the Hungarian government, rushed to the Serb villagers, and massacred everyone they could reach. When they could not catch up with the Serbian outlaws who committed these horrifying, Balkan sins, the troops destroyed the furnishings of the Serb church. I learnt all this from an authentic source, reading the memoir of an Austrian colonel, Count Leopold Kolowrat. According to him, even the Serb commander was shocked at the events.

On August 19th, the Hungarian army in Bácska, by this time strengthened, was ordered by Defense Secretary Lázár Mészáros to lay siege to Szenttamás again. The assault started from three different directions, the villages Kiskér, Verbász, and Óbecse. Though the attacking parties of the 2nd infantry regiment, led by

Colonel Bakonyi and Lieutenant-Colonel Aulich, succeeded in breaching the fortification, the attack failed again because of the tough resistance of the Serbs.

The main reason for the victory of the Serbs in Szenttamás is the fact that the rebel troops consisted of veterans; experienced frontier guards; and trained Serbian volunteers; while the Hungarian soldiers were mostly untrained draftees.

Owing to this, the third attack on September 21, proved also unsuccessful, although it had been organized under Lázár Mészáros' leadership. The repeated failure of the Hungarian soldiers strengthened to a great extent the rebels' confidence and martial spirit.

On April 1, 1849, Mór Perczel's division of 7,000 battle hardened soldiers laid siege to Szenttamás, which was defended by some four thousand Serb frontier guardsmen.

The village, situated on the banks of the Ferenc Canal, was approached at dawn on the 3rd of April by the two columns of Mór Perczel's forces, who came from two directions, east and south.

One of the columns came from Verbász, under the leadership of Colonel Miklós Gál, the other one was commanded by Miklós Perczel, from Kisbér.

Before the battle the dark image of the last year's atrocity in Földvár, the image of the 37 beheaded Hungarian children in front of the Catholic altar; had been circulating among the Hungarian soldiers. Though few of them had participated in the reoccupation of Földvár, all of them became furious while marching toward Szenttamás.

The battle started with the pounding of artillery at seven in the morning. The Serbian frontier guards beat back three charges of the Hungarian infantry. The long lasting gun fire and the bayonet charges proved unsuccessful. Nevertheless, Miklós Perczel at last managed to occupy the bridge-head. Taking advantage of this opportunity, Sándor Földváry entered the fortification, flourishing a flag, accompanied by national guardsmen from Szeged.

An awful hand to hand fight followed. The Serbs wanted to flee over the bridge, but the determined Hungarian soldiers, were chasing them and threw most of them over the railing of the bridge.

At another location, Gál's column was unable to break the desperate resistance for a very long time, and he could only succeed after Miklós Perczel had entered the village.

Since the soldiers from Szeged were successful, the other Hungarian troops could occupy the right, then the left sides of the fortification. Then the battle raged higher against the frontier guardsmen, who tried to seek a place to hide in the village. At last it ended with a sweeping victory. The Hungarians cut down all the captured Serbs, as neither side gave mercy. Upon seeing beheaded Hungarian corpses on the main square of the village, the Hungarian soldiers fought with an even more ruthless fury.

After the bloody struggle, about two thousand Serb frontier guards were found dead on the battle field. The Hungarian casualties came to 200.

According to the Serbian notion of valor, the villagers of Srbobran, which was renamed Szenttamás in 1941, could not have surrendered to the arriving Hungarian troops without putting up a fight.

The Hungarian soldiers were fired at in the streets or from attics. They sometimes fired back, but were not always hitting the place where the snipers were shooting from.

During the days of the Hungarian entry in 1941, ninety-two Serbs from Szenttamás died.

In the following months the Hungarians interned twelve people, accused with illegal subversive activity and the counter-intelligence corps arrested and took away twenty-one villagers.

Without any investigation, we can easily assume that among the dead, the interned, and those accused of espionage, there may have been those who were completely innocent and had to suffer despite their innocence, says a Yugoslavian summary made in 1946.

No one can tell whether the bloodshed of 1849 or that of 1941 created a more ardent memory for the villagers in Szenttamás. Obviously, in the fall of 1944, mainly the latter one would be more vividly remembered by concerned families or relatives.

According to the martial morals of the partisans, "the liberators of the people", the revenge could not have been avoided.

Pál Süge is one of the few witnesses of the revenge who dared to verify his testimony by giving his name. Obviously, since he fled to a Western country, he was not afraid that the retaliation could reach him. Therefore, he told the Serbian national secret. In 1944, Pál Süge was 21, and at this most vulnerable age, he succeded in hiding away from the murderous Serbian guns in his native village.

"In October 1944, when the Hungarian and German army units evacuated Szenttamás, the Russian troops and Tito's partisans marched in immediately. Then there were 18 thousand villagers, now only 15 thousand people live here. Three thousand Hungarians were either killed or carried off. The partisans led the groups of captured men to the old Serbian cemetery, where the victims were forced to dig their own graves. Having finished working, they were shot dead while standing in their graves. These were common graves. The following groups buried the dead, then they had to dig new graves for themselves. The executions continued for four or five days; each night two or three groups were executed. A group consisted of 150-200 people. The length of the graves was 15-20 m, the width was some 7 m. There are 4 or 5 mass graves like that. There are smaller common graves, with 15-20 corpses in them.

I can explain why they were massacred with the help of an example. My cousin's wife, in her seventh month of pregnancy, was carried off at night, then they beat her severely, and shot her dead in the cemetery together with the other victims. Her only guilt was that her husband was a Hungarian soldier and an arrow-cross man (i.e. member of the Hungarian Nazi party), though he did not hold any office. A woman, between 40-45 years old, crawled out of the common grave, but she bled to death about 100 metres from there. By the next day, hungry stray dogs had torn her body to pieces. Those who had Serbian enemies were all slaughtered, including their families. All those whose Chetnik sons had been convicted by the Hungarian authorities had their revenge."

Though all Hungarian villagers in Szenttamás suffered a great deal during the reign of terror, all of them cannot be included among the victims, as some emigrated from there, or died natural deaths. So our sad summary does not have an exact final result.

According to even a conservative estimate, the number of the executed is above one thousand. The greatest possible number is around two thousand. The unrestrained killing and most of the executions lasted four days. Thereafter, Hungarians were murdered in Szenttamás only occasionally.

Three common graves were in the cemetery, but there were other graves at the lumber mill, and at the cloister.

An eight-year-old girl had accidentally witnessed the slaughter unobserved, and told her parents what she had seen. The neighbors heard the child's report, too. Rumor had it that the innocent little girl had "harmful" news. The next day the partisans took away the little witness and executed her.

In 1941, seven Serb men died by rifle fire in Bácsföldvár, and another seven were arrested by the counter-intelligence in the following years.

In 1944, in the same village seventy innocent Hungarian men were led to the bank of the Tisza and shot, so that their bodies fell into the river near Gyöngy Island.

None of the remaining Hungarians in Földvár remember the 1848 beheading of Hungarian children by the rebel Serbian Frontierguards....

SZIVÁC

At the beginning of the 1940s, seven Serbian men from Szivác were imprisoned and investigated by the Hungarian counter-intelligence. Szivác was inhabited by three nationalities, who had lived together in peace for centuries.

"...I am determined to send you a roll including the names of those who were executed (annihilated) in the morning, on November 1, 1944, because I have been a victim of atrocities myself. It is true that because of the repeated threats all this has been taboo for me, and I did not dare to tell anyone but my family. Honestly, the fear is still alive in me. It is true that newspapers are beginning to publish data concerning these events gradually, but the survivors still do not dare to speak, give their names, or make exact data known, because there is no "democracy", no human right to freedom. Only the name has changed; the power has remained the same.

I was born in February 1923, in Ó-Szivác (now Sivac). Then the village was part of Zombor, now it is attached to Kula.

Before and during World War II, the composition of the village was approximately the following: Ó- and Uj-Szivác was one at that time, but 95% of the inhabitants in Uj-Szivác were German, and Ó-Szivác was mixed. The entire population came to 14,000 among them 8,000-8,500 Germans, 1,200-1,300 Hungarians, and about 4,800 Serbs.

When the Hungarian troops withdrew from the village on the 12th and 13th of October, 1944, the "communist" commando was formed at once, and they began arresting people (men) on the 15th. Two armed so-called "partisans" carried off my father and me on the 17th. I was led to a many-storied barn in Ó-Szivác, where they had already arrested 40-50 local Hungarians and some Germans. My father was driven to Uj-Szivác, where there were only 10-12 men at the village hall, since the partisans did not take any more people there.

Where I was, additional people were brought in. A couple of us were let free, but on the 1st of November, at nine in the morning a group of strangers, called "partisans", burst into the house. They told us they were from Csurog, and that they would shoot, but they just beat us. Most of them struck us with rifle butts, in the head, in the shoulder, up and down. I lost consciousness because of the blows, and recovered my senses in the afternoon, but I was unable to move even then. The barn (magazine) was at the end of the garden of the Serb school. The Serb teacher rushed to my mother and told her that I was dead. My mother was running to and fro, and tried everything to get me out of there. At last, with much difficulty, the doctor came to see me. I received an injection from the village doctor, at least I was told so, and regained my consciousness at about five. But I still was not able to move. At six an official came with the doctor and with another injection. They put me on a stretcher, and handed me over in the street to two youngsters. They carried me home, but my mother was not allowed to see me. I could get home only this way, with a fracture of a rib, unable to see, to hear, or feel anything. By the next morning the ten people in the barn in Uj-Szivác had all disappeared. On November 2, we learnt that they had all been executed on that night. My father was among them.

Two months later we found out that my cousin had escaped from the Serb cemetery, where all the others were massacred.

At the end of December, I was driven to a private infirmary in Hódság, now Odzaci. I was treated so efficiently that in two or three months I could get about again. I stayed in Hódság till 1955, when we moved to Szabadka; I still live here. I don't own a thing at home, in Ó-Szivác; they confiscated all I had. My mother was interned in a camp (lager) without a proper judicial process, and released after half a year. She was allowed to live in our house until her death, that's all they permitted her. Later on she moved in with us in Szabadka.

It was only the two of us who escaped from the barn, where 73 men were locked up. My cousin still lives in Moravica.

Dear Mr. Cseres, if you make use of anything written down here please do not mention my name, and burn the letter. I would like present-day generations to be aware of what happened to innocent people who were not even interrogated or sentenced. All that took place then is still considered taboo by the authorities.

The roll of the executed victims;

Ferencz Alföldi, Lajos Bacsó (innkeeper), János Baka, János Balogh (wool spinner), István Bocskovics, József Bódis, Lajos Bódis, István Breznyák, József Breznyák, András Búza, Peter Czifra, András Czifra (lumberman), an unknown male from Csurog, János Dávid, János Daruhalmi (tanner), Mihály Domján, István Dragity (tradesman), István Drobnyik, János Farkas, János Farkas, Lajos Farkas, Pál Farkas, István Farkas (bricklayer), József Horváth, András Horváth, Antal Juhász, István Klebecsko, András Lavró, Mihály Mándity, János Mezei (cartwright), Mihály Merkel, Mihály Merkel, Jenő Mérő, Ferencz Molnár, Antal Mudri, József Nagy, József Nagy Jr., Ferencz Nagy, Imre Nagy, József Papp (corn buyer), Mihály Pavlik, Sándor Rácz (Chubby, musician), István Rácz (musician), Péter Rigó, Péter Siflis, István Siflis, Károly Skorutyák (tailor), Antal Skorutyák (owner of a small dairy), Adám Strikovics (joiner), Imre Szalai, János Szalai, István Szabó Péter Szobek, István Tóth, Mihály Tokodi, Mihály Tokodi Jr., Péter Turi, Péter Uglik, János Városi (deputy clerk), István Zsellér - all Hungarians.

An unknown man from Cservenka, Jakab Burger, Johann Gubola, Anton Hunsinger, Anton Modritsch (tradesman), Ferdinand Stieb, Anton Teehr, Heinrich Winterstein - they were the German victims.

Pero Czigány, a Serb horse-dealer.

The people in Szivác were, and still are, so frightened that they did not dare to celebrate a mass for their dead, or to bring some flowers to the mass grave.

No one knows for what capricious reason the killers had by forcing the men dig the large common grave in the shape of a "M" (for abbreviated Magyar in Hungarian), in an area between the Catholic (Hungarian) and the Serb cemeteries.

In the large village barn the murderers treated their victims in an oddly ambiguous way. Beside torturing and beating people severely, they allowed a doctor to go and see a young boy who was supposed to be dead. They are said to have let the captured teamsters go home for one or two days to provide for their horses, though these men were looked after strictly, and were ordered to return.

Those who were willing to join the Petőfi Brigade and fight against the "fascists" were released and directed to the organization center, Topolya. On the other hand, the partisans cut off all fingers of Jenő Mérő, the veterinarian's son, with an axe, just because he did not want to join them.

Sándor Simó, the ranger, did not accept either alternative, and ran away at the right moment, unarmed, squeezing out the eyes of his armed partisan guard.

Our correspondent's cousin reports on his daring escape as follows;

"Stripped to the skin; wired together in pairs (I was tied with my father); we were led to the cemetery; and ordered to stand with our backs to the graves, so that they did not have to bother to put our corpses there. It was pitch-dark; only the barrels of machine guns told us that behind each barrel a partisan was standing ready to kill. I whispered to my father, "I will undo the wire and we can go!" My father nodded affirmatively, but he surely did not believe that he could be as youthfully brisk as I was. Having my wrists set free, I knew the partisan officer would order fire in an instant. With a swift movement I signaled my father to escape, and shoving aside the gun pointed at me I punched the partisan on the cheek with my free right hand (I was in good shape then). He tottered and was so astonished that he failed to fire his gun. For a few moments, the others did not comprehend what had happened. I could easily find my way about in the cemetery, so the rare pursuing rifle-fire hit only tombs and possibly my slower father. I was running toward the farm where my father-in-law was a lease-holder renting the land from a German farmer. Though naked, I was recognized by the dogs, and I got a change of clothes from my father-in-law . Trying to avoid being found, I left the farm for Monrovia. Feeling secure, I returned to Szivác on New Year's Eve.

Soon there was a rumor going about that I had escaped and returned home. My mother, a widow by then, was unable to keep the secret.

Two weeks later, Branko Bikicskics, then the chief communist in Szivác, ordered my arrest. I got a heavy beating because I had escaped from the cemetery. Being considered a deserter, I was escorted to the military authority in Zombor. I acknowledged being a deserter, as I fled from the Hungarian army in September. They enlisted me in the Yugoslavian army; that is how I became a Serb "volunteer". However, in my dreams I keep running. I dream that I grab my father's hand; separating the two closest partisans with kicks; I thrust aside the gun pointed at my father, and he runs away with me. By the time I wake up, my forehead is beaded with sweat."

ADORJÁN; NADRIJÁN, THE UNFORTUNATE

The village of Adorján was given a new name signifying "unfortunate" by the Serbian administrative authority in memory of the events of 1918.

On a pleasant morning during the takeover, two easy-going Serbian soldiers on a spree, took a short trip from Kanizsa to well-known, prosperous village of Adorján. They had a little food and drink, for free of course, and probably also happened to meet some waitresses who were happy to satisfy their desire for women without violence. They were occasionally firing their weapons into the ceiling of the bar, for the sake of maintaining their reputation.

The two heroes' bullyboy notoriety had spread in the village. The bar-owner heaved a sigh of relief, when at dusk the two tipsy soldiers made ready to set out for Kanizsa by carriage. They found a man keeping horses and frightened him after his initial refusal to lend them his horses. It was late and he was afraid that his horses would be stolen; they might even shoot him on the way. In the end, however, a very different result transpired. He hitched the horses to the carriage for the benefit of the two drunks. The carriage was standing in the yard and the two "travellers" climbed on board, keeping their guns between their knees. The horse-owner was an ex-serviceman and kept a gun at home under the crib. Mortally afraid of being killed by these drunks on their way to Kanizsa, he shot his boisterous guests in the head. That night, with the help of his neighbors and ex-comrades-in-arms, he took the two bodies to the Tisza river and threw them in.

Within the next few days, the Serbian military commander ordered his men to try to find the two missing persons. What had taken place at Adorján somehow came to light. The army burned several parts of the village. The villagers were prohibited from dousing the flames. When five of them ignored this command, the soldiers shot them in cold blood. Furthermore, fifty men were taken away from the village.

"In 1941, two "dobrovoljacs" were captured in this village by Hungarian soldiers. The two unfortunate men were on their way home from the Serbian army, probably to Velebit. A third, a Jewish physician, was also captured. They wanted to shoot the three men then and there. My father warned the sergeant that he should do everything legally and before a court. The Hungarian officer went to him and said, "You, why are you defending them?

Are you a Jew too?" The three men were executed. This was the only bloody event in Adorján in 1941.

In November, 1944, the relatives of these two dobrovoljacs may also have returned to revenge the spirits of their fallen dead.

On about the 30th of October, terrible Serbian and Hungarian cries could be heard coming from Bánát on the opposite bank of the Tisza."Get a boat! We want to cross the river!" They were partisans. No one moved because there was shooting everywhere around the river. The bullets were hissing and fizzing over our heads. As yet, no one told them that the fishermen had knocked out the bottom of the boats to prevent the use or theft of them by the opposing armies.

Our house looked out over the main street and our garden, which was long and quite large backed onto the Tisza river. Rifle fire from the opposite side was whizzing over us, whenever I could pluck up enough courage to look out for only a short time, I was almost able to see the firing partisans. They were shouting for more than an hour. When the shooting was at its height two Cossacks came on horseback and shouted "cease fire". It was obvious that they were afraid of losing their horses, and spiced up their order with some Russian curses. The Bánát people, however, did not cease fire and so the Cossacks set up their machine gun and started to shoot at the partisans from the end of our garden. Seeing this, the partisans held their fire and set out on foot for Kanizsa.

The next day a body of partisan troops arrived from Kanizsa. They announced immediately that everyone had to gather in the market square. Two or three hundred of us had gathered there at the appointed time including a lot of women and children. This surprised the partisans who encircled the crowd. My understanding was from what they were saying that they had planned to execute the men in front of the church then and there, but now they seemed to change their minds and they blithely announced that everyone had to continue with their daily routine. They shot dead the village idiot in the cemetery because he couldn't answer their questions as they wanted.After that they were shooting around on the church square aimlessly and later started to go from door to door.

Jurisics Miso from Kanizsa who we had knew came to our house and told us or rather whispered to us briefly:

"The farmer must hide", so my father disappeared immediately.

Then a stranger came in looking for the farmer. We told him that he had gone to work in the fields, as had been ordered. Then he sat down and asked for a drink. My mother sent me to the bar to get half a liter of rum. When I came back and gave it to him, he took a swig from the bottle and offered some to me. I told him that I didn't want to drink, especially not rum, but it was no good saying anything, finally I had to have a drop. He said that someone had fired at one of their commanders and that his left hand was hurt, and that our village would have trouble because of it. "The wounded man" was our partisan, Jurisics, whose left hand was wrapped in a white handkerchief soaked with the village idiot's blood.

The stranger left us without taking anything.

From the barn, where I had hidden myself, I could see that the shopkeeper, Antal Laczkó had been out of his shop, taken to the the market square in the company of several others. Almost all of the farmers had been driven out of their houses by partisans into the square in front of the church.

After an hour I could see fifty or sixty men from Adorján marching in pairs accompanied by the partisans towards Kanizsa. These were mostly from the end of the village. There my Uncle Gyula Miluticsovics, despite his Serbian name and Mr. Bakota, the village teacher. Someone, perhaps trying to escape wanted to open the small gate but it was locked.

There were seventeen partisans who passed in Indian file along the side of our house ready to shoot if necessary.

As they passed by, I tried to follow them from our garden. Soon I realised that they were not going towards Kanizsa. They were going to the bank of the Tisza River. I was afraid of being spotted, so I carefully made my way back among the corn stalks and finally I jumped into the ditch dug on the ridge by my father to protect our garden from the roots of the trees in the neighbour's garden. I was about two-hundred metres away from the Tisza while the wild firing continued. It could not have been more than half an hour later, when the partisans came back in groups congratulating themselves in very loud voices, enthusiastically praising each other for their impressive "shooting". All night long we could hear cries for help becoming weaker and weaker from the river, from the farm which stood twenty metres away from the river; none of us was brave enough to go there.

I could hardly sleep that night, but at dawn I took courage and walked through our garden down to the Tisza. I saw pieces of clothing, clogs, short overcoats, fur-caps, hats and caps on the ten metre high bank. Then I looked down to the hole by the water and I saw four bodies half-sunk. I only recognized my Uncle Gyula Miluticsovics and Antal Bakota, the teacher, from their clothes.

Then from the farm, Márta Felhő ran up barefooted and began to wail in a dreadful way, when she found her husband Lukács's hat. Lukács Apczi's nickname was Felhő (Cloud).

Uncle Pista Gubec (also a nickname) had looked on from the corn-field while the massacre took place. The men were lined up in twos on the bank of the river and the partisans had taken aim at their heads in this way; that was why they had to remove their hats and caps.

At about noon a lot of women set out with food in baskets to try to find their starved loved ones as soon they knew where their men had been taken. I was the only one who could tell them that it was no use going there.

I have never heard, before or since, such heart-piercing wailing as when these women found the clothes of their husbands, sons or fathers.

That same afternoon we pulled the corpses out of the water. The third whom I was able to recognise was Uncle Pista Ladóczki, another one of my relatives. The fourth was István Tandari, a wealthy farmer. Not all of the four men died immediately after the firing, three of them bled to death in the shallow water.

The next day saw the five dead bodies still lying in the cemetery, since there were no coffins. The fifth unburied body was the village idiot, the "faulty" Antal Bakota left five orphans behind him. The top of his skull was missing and I had to shoo the hens of the grave-digger away because they were picking at the bloody brain.

The partisan commander who we knew, warned Firányi, the parish priest in front of the church;

"If you love your life, get out of here!"; the priest ran away to his house and hid as quickly as he could, probably in the loft.

János Bicskei, the thirty-two year old teacher, was lined up because his hands were too white and clean. Although he had been educated in Belgrade and could speak Serbian quite well, it didn't help. He was suffering from tuberculosis and had not served as a soldier.

The unluckiest of all, however, was Sándor Lukács, who had been taken prisoner by the Russians falling behind the retreating Hungarian troops, but had somehow managed to escape. He had just arrived home after three years of war. He was just about to take a bath and shave, when the partisans took him away.

Because of the chaos and the bombing, Mihály Radák, a 65-year-old teacher from Szeged, had moved in here with Apczi. He was destined to die here on the bank of the Tisza also.

One of the victims of Adorján had got stuck nearby in some roots under the water. István Bácskai, his body turned up in the Tisza six months later. He was identified from his leather belt.

Of the fifty-six victims of Adorján only one, Imre Csanádi was who could be regarded in any way as guilty. He had participated in the execution of the two dobrovoljacs and the Jewish physician in 1941.

Jurisics Miso, the commander warned Uncle Gyula to hide away. Gyula Miluticsovics followed his advice, but when a partisan turned up looking for the farmer and was on the point of shooting the snarling guard dog, my uncle Gyula came forward to protect his dog.

Later we asked this commander why he had participated in the massacre. He replied that if he had not, then he would have been executed too.The following year the commander of the massacre in Adorján, Radakovics from Kanizsa, was accused of the massacre of 56 innocent men. He was entenced to forced labour for twelve months. A rare example. One of his fellows, Knjezevic, got off with six months forced labour. That's how cheap the Hungarian lives were worth.

At the beginning of December, all young men over eighteen years of age were summoned before the recruiting commission in Kanizsa. From there through Kishegyes, we marched in ranks of four accompanied by armed partisans towards Topolya to join the Petőfi Brigade to fight for communist Yugoslavia.

In Kishegyes, a young wife caught up with us bringing some food. She approached her husband marching in the ranks and wanted to pass the food to him. A vigilant partisan shot her.

I escaped from Topolya, because I didn't want to die as a member of the Petőfi Brigade. I crossed the Hungarian border at the end of December."

Another man from Adorján, remembering these events, says that in the high bank of the Tisza the "holes" are now totally different from those of that time, because rocks have been put under the bank against the ravine.

As far as he knew, not everyone that lined up for execution received a mortal wound. Some were even able to jump into the water uninjured. The partisans, however, jumped down into the tied-up and half-sinking boats and shot them from there No one was able to count how many men from Adorján were shot into the Tisza river.

Only the postman in Oromhegyes (Tresnjevac) could provide any facts He had heard a partisan calling to his fellow in Adorján;

"We sent the birds to the Tisza."
The partisan in Tresnjevac had asked;
"How many birds were there ?"
"There were about fifty", answered the other Serb partisan from Adorján.

Mention must be made of a number of events of 1941, which may be regarded as having preceded what took place in Adorján. At the end of March or the beginning of April a Serbian river gunboat moored near Adorján. A Serbian officer went often to the village to drink and to get to know the people. It was known in the village that the Hungarian occupation is impending. This friendly officer was eventually invited to a party, where they got him drunk and then confined him for several hours or perhaps even days, then the warship was ordered to sail. The hosts released the Serbian officer who was now sober and he began desperately to run after the warship which was now going away from the bank. It is said that the Serbian partisans spoke of this event as a crime.

It is also said that the teacher from Adorján begged for his life desperately, because of his five children. No pity was shown to him, however, as he was told that at least now he would not be able to increase the number of Hungarians.

The following 56 men were executed on the bank of the Tisza in Adorján;

1. Lukács Apczi, 33
2. Antal Bakota, 44
3. Miklós Bánszki, 38
4. János Bicskei, 32
5. József Bicskei, 41
6. József Bicskei, 19
7. István Bicskei, 38
8. Sándor Bognár, 36
9. István Borsos, 22
10. József Borsos, 22
11. Lajos Dukai, 38
12. Lukács Dukai, 45
13. Vilmos Gandis 30
14. Gyula Horváth, 40
15. Orbán Kis, 25
16. János Kocsis, 63
17. Ferenc Kovács, 27
18. Gyula Körmőczi, 23

29. József Pörzsölt, 33
30. Mihály Radák, 69
31. József Hemete, 38
32. Ferenc Rózsa, 24
33. István Sarnyai, 44
34. István Sándor, 42
35. Géza Sándor, 35
36. Lukács Sándor, 24
37. János Sétai, 61
38. István Sindeles, 30
39. Ferenc Szabó, 44
40. Pál Szabados, 34
41. Jakab Szecsei, 39
42. Lukács Szecsei, 56
43. Ferenc Sziveri, 19
44. Pál Takács, 36
45. István Tandari, 46
46. István Vajda, 66

19. Simon Körmőczi, 23
20. Antal Laczkó, 24
21. István Ladóczki, 62
22. Pál Lengyel, 37
23. Péter Magda, 37
24. Gyula Miluticsovics
25. János Nagy, 37
26. János Németh, 37
27. János Pásztor, 32
28. József Pásztor, 34

47. Jakab Vajda, 42
48. Károly Varga, 31
49. Miklós Vajda, 23
50. Ferenc Vörös, 36
51. Ferenc Zöldi, 29
52. Kelemen Filiszter, 39
53. Zoltán Kocsis, 38
54. István Balassa 27
55. Imre Csanadi, 32
56. Albert Gazdag, 50

KANIZSA

"In 1941, when the Hungarian troops marched in to Kanizsa, the Bagi lads and Lajos Barta beat up about twelve Serbian prisoners at the Town Hall. Bato Knazsavity was beaten so black and blue that I could hardly recognize him, but he survived to take his revenge on 300 Hungarians in in 1944.

It is said that some Serbians were executed during the war in 1941. It is possible, but I know only of the one executed at the Town Hall. He was the lame tailor who had shouted idiotically that he wanted to eat a meal of the flesh of Hungarians. However it is possible that this man should have been taken to the Mental Hospital rather than executed. It's also true that most of the partisans would have deserved the same.

The Russian troops crossing the Tisza marched into Kanizsa on October 7, 1944. There was neither a battle nor a massacre, but every woman was raped despite the fact that most of them could speak Serbian. Murderous partisans from Bánát also came with the Russian troops; their leaders were Niklo Radovics and Szvetozár Knezevics Bacsa. It was announced that if a Russian or Serbian person were to be hurt and subsequently die, a hundred Hungarians would meet the same fate. After a number of days, a Serbian soldier did happen to be shot in Pál Mányi's bar. Fortunately ,before he died, he admitted that he had been shot by Dusan Tatics, a fellow Serb.

At the end of October or the beginning of November, people began to be picked up one by one on the basis of a list. Whoever was able to do so fled to Szeged. We could not sleep for weeks. I put my bed underneath the kitchen window leaving a small opening, so that if they came, I could jump through the window, and run away to Martonos or even farther away. Those rounded up were put in the Town Hall prison and knocked about on the basis of whatever pretext came into their interrogators' minds. For example; "Have you ever been a levente?" "Sure, I have." There was a powerful punch to the chin. "You also have been a levente, and you are a Serbian!" There were harder punches and kicks to the body of the poor Hungarian.

Most of those taken were beaten to death in the cellar of the Town Hall. The dead bodies were driven by carts to the Island at night. There the corpses were laid out unburied and covered with lime for days. Then the partisans gathered some people to dig ditches, pits, lug corpses and bury them any old way; it was all the same to them. Finally some of them were also shot dead."

It is characteristic of the work these unlucky men were forced to undertake. Decayed parts of human bodies were dug up by stray dogs near the park as late as 1975.

Some of those were not beaten to death in the cellar of the Town Hall, were shot near the pathway leading to the Tisza; others into the river; or on its bank near the dike. They were also buried there. There are two mass-graves razed to the ground in this area. Later on relatives put crosses on the two graves, but these were removed by the authorities. One of the common graves was next to the path, while the other was near the bank of the Tisza, 150-200 metres to the south between the Tisza and the dike. No one has the courage to dig up the graves overgrown with weeds and bushes to rebury the bodies decently.

Most of the murderers were Serbians who had lived in Kanizsa before 1941. Besides those mentioned above, Alexander Oluski nicknamed Saco and Dusan Ugranov, nicknamed Dusko were also involved in the massacre there. The wife of Ugranov was Dragice Kardevan who was the secretary of the commander of OZNA. They were the ones who asked the younger prisoners if they wanted to join the Petőfi-brigade. When everyone of them accepted this offer just to save their lives, the Serbian Kanizsa people beat them to death with even greater pleasure. The gesture and the comment made by Dusko as a protest, when he saw the three-hundredth corpse, were not contrary; "Comrades, let's finish it; if we kill every Hungarian, who will work for us?" A real humanitarian...

It made no difference for those who had been marked for execution, whether they had been fighters in the class struggle or members of any political party whatever; what mattered was their ethnic origin.

In the first few days, a few illusory personal touches characterised the events. Female relatives (wives, mothers, sisters) of the prisoners attempted to carry some food to them. It was passed on to the prisoners by the executioner's assistants and so it wasn't possible to see anyone personally. The most "honorable" action of the Serbian partisans was that they gave back the food which had been brought for men who had been beaten to death. They said that the relative had been transported somewhere else.

The third wave of executions, which demanded only 22 dead, came on November 22nd. It was a Yugoslavian holiday. Dusko and his friends celebrated the holiday with the humorous idea, as they thought of executing 22 Hungarians to fit the date.

Only one man, Antal Dobó (Tóni), who had been a member of the party, dared to protest against this terrible idea. After he had failed to prevent the "ceremony", he and another strong fellow buried those executed to save their bodies from the pigs of the forester.

Saco Oluski, together with the partisans of Adorján were held responsible   for the three hundred victims. He is said to have been condemned to death, but the sentence was never carried out.

We might also mention the case of Dusan Ugranov; he had lived with a guilty conscience since 1944. He had a nervous breakdown and as a psychiatric patient he would shout; "Help! Save me! The Hungarians will come and execute me!" He had a persecution complex and a clouded mind; he died in 1970.

The OZNA officer, who exhumed a mass-grave of 60 corpses in 1946, blew out his own brains because of the shock and under the weight of responsibility.

The cruellest killers had already moved to other parts of the country at the time of the first legal action taken in relation to these crimes.

Under the influence of articles which have been published recently, the less important killers are moving south, while the administrative positions in Kanizsa are being occupied by "reliable" non-Hungarians from Serbia in the name of "reconciliation".

The long list of the Hungarian dead in Kanizsa has not yet been completed.

ÓBECSE AND VERONICA'S VEIL

If we ask the Hungarians living in Óbecse, what happened there in October and November 1944 almost everyone will remember the terrible torture and killing of the priest first, and only then the torture and disappearance of their relatives. The number of murdered Hungarians is put at 600 by the villagers. The full list has not yet been compiled.

The cruelty of the massacres indicated personal revenge. In most cases there was no direct relationship between the killers and their victims.

When the Hungarians reoccupied this area in 1941, seven Serbians from Óbecse died. Another died when a gendarme was searching for hidden fugitives in the loft of Ragacs the lumber merchant. A hiding Serbian shot him in the forehead. He had to pay for this along with the others living in the same house.

Forty people including three engineers were arrested by counter-intelligence. A transmitter had been found with each of the engineers. They said that during the raid 206 Serbian villagers from Óbecse died. (The information came from Yugoslavia in 1946). Probably some of these people died because of their Serbian nationalist feelings. Csurog and Zsablya Becse were rarely mentioned.

In 1944, revenge started against Hungarians, who didn't show any resistance, with the slogan: "Two Hungarians were to die for every Serbian." The Serbians were not interested in finding the guilty, nor did they initiate proper legal action.

The locations of the massacres were the Central Coffee House and the multi-story hotel building. No one who entered the building left alive. Even in December, the massacre was still continuing. Anyone left alive at the Central was taken to the cellar of the music school; they showed no signs of life any more.

Hungarians living on farms were also gathered and many men were shot. Many conflicting estimates have been given concerning the number of the dead ranging from 100 to 600. It was enough to be Hungarian or to speak out in any way against communism or the Serbians to be considered guilty, a war criminal, and to die for it.

Abbot Ferenc Petrányi was taken away from his home on October 9, by young partisan women. On the way to the Centrál, they beat the 65-year-old priest. He was forced to make a "confession" of alleged wrong doings against the Serbians, but he felt not even a glimmer of hatred towards them. Every part of his body and face were beaten black and blue and his jaw was smashed. A partisan woman named Zorka from Zombor was the cruelest of all. The naked priest was fastened to a board; then they jumped on his belly, chest and genitals from a table in hobnailed boots; he was practically disembowelled. When he died from his wounds on October 14, he was thrown out of an upstairs window onto the cobbled court; the cause of death was given as suicide. (But what need was there for justification?)

One of the partisan women was said to have been burdened by the memory of his murder throughout her life. She became neurotic and she would frequently mention the priest's name in her nightmares. Those who believe in divine justice should know that the other four partisan girls, but especially Zorka, died in a very unfortunate manner.

The niece of the priest, whose husband was an engineer and a soldier during the war, lived with her two year old son, her mother and the priest's sister. In a five room residence. The niece, who was then 38, remembers the events:

"As if my Uncle Ferenc Petrányi had felt the oncoming danger, he was working at his desk that night. He had already felt the shadow of his death the same evening. The partisan women called for him at half past three. My son, whom my uncle loved very much was still sleeping; my uncle wasn't even allowed to kiss his forehead in farewell. He was seen no more. We heard that he was being kept under arrest in the town hall or at the Centrál.

We enquired whether or not we could send some food to him. The following day we sent some food in a small basket with our maid. I put a white handkerchief under the plate. The maid waited for the empty basket outside the Centrál. The handkerchief was in it, but it was all bloody. We thought that his nose had been bleeding as usual.

We sent the maid to take his lunch next day, too. Then I put a big, white table-cloth under the plates. Then the maid came back with the basket and we looked at the table-cloth. There was the mark of a tortured, bloody face on it; it was just like Veronica's veil.

After that we could not send any more food to my uncle. We heard that he had jumped out of the window and died at once. We were asked to send a coffin with one of the undertaker's assistants. We did so, but we weren't allowed to go there. The only thing we were allowed to do was to accompany the hearse with the closed coffin on it; they would not let us see my uncle's body.

We stopped for a brief prayer in front of the church. My mother didn't come, just the maid and us, along with an armed partisan with the driver.

With the help of the parishioners of Becse, my mother, a Yugoslavian citizen, could stay in the village. She had a nice marble tombstone placed on the grave of my uncle and a moving poem engraved on it. My mother would have remembered the lines of the poem if she were still alive, because now it cannot be read. The whole poem was chiselled off the tomb.

My little son and I were taken to the silk factory with orphaned Székely children from a near-by village. They didn't know what had happened to their parents."

EARLY PARTISANS WITH LILY-WHITE HANDS

"My father was drafted as a Hungarian soldier from Becse on Sunday, September 16 1944. My mother was left with her sons,

17 year old Károly and 8 year old Gyula. They lived on a rented farm not far away from the Bogdány farm in Határjárás. They had been living there for a long time and had a very good relationship with the owner, Mr. Cseszák. Cseszák, a clerk. He took up this post after the arrival of the Hungarians. He lived on Zöldfás Street, near the entrance to the market, he was divorced and lived with his son. He was considered to be a very good man in Becse.

When my father, József Kovács, was drafted, he hired a couple to help my mother cut the hay. It was September 18th, at eight o'clock in the evening, and they had just gone to bed. My mother and her sons were frightened when someone began knocking on the door. They thought that the couple living in the stable wanted to break into the house. My mother picked up her smallest son who was still sleeping and carried him with her. The older boy went ahead of her through the next room. The boy jumped out of the window, but came back immediately and shouted:

"Mum, there are a lot of people here." At that precise moment he was shot through the heart and died at once. My mother was shot at five times, three of the shots hit the boy in her arms. One bullet grazed her just beside the ear and the other next to her eye.

Then the shooting stopped and the partisans came to my mother and asked her where Cseszák was. My mother answered that he was living in the town.

"We're looking for him", they told her. My mother said that we were living here now. The wagon in the yard had a small registration plate on it, with my father's name on it. The Serbian partisans numbered a hundred or more, a lot of guns with them. According to my mother, all of them had fine, smooth hands. They were not peasants or workers but clerks and other white collar workers, young and middle-aged. There was a Hungarian woman among them who asked my mother;

"Do you know who we are?" My mother said that she did not. "We are the troops of liberation. In two weeks the Russians will arrive and we will liberate Becse." "I don't care, I would just like one thing, please, bring my sons into the house", she said, as she looked at her dead sons lying on the ground.

"Not there", they were pointing at the house from which my mother and her sons had come."Take them in there then", my mother said, pointing to the summer kitchen. They took the dead bodies there.

Meanwhile they went into the house and took everything we had away with them. The curtains were torn away; clothes and bedding were wrapped in other bedding, so they could be taken away more easily. Some days later one of these packs was found in the nearby corn field.

The only dress left for my mother was the one she wore and she had to borrow one from her mother, so that she could go to the funeral. The sons' best clothes were at my father's grandparents' in Becse, so they were buried in the clothes they had been wearing when they were murdered. The partisans were there for a while and told my mother that she shouldn't go into the house before morning. My mother did not notice that she had been robbed in the meanwhile.

Then the partisans set off through the corn field towards another farm, where Cseszák lived. There were three Cseszák farms in the countryside and ours was the first the partisans visited. That evening they broke into another Cseszák farm and there they castrated another Cseszák who died on the spot.

They took someone with them as a hostage and he told me all this (later he hid under the leafes of a big pumpkin in the corn field and managed to escape that way).

The partisan who shot my brothers regretted it later saying; "Why did I kill them when I knew their father and grandfather." Another partisan tried to comfort him by saying; "Don't regret it; two Hungarians less!" The murderer lived some distance from our grandparents' house. Later we lived there too, in one of the houses on Marshal Tito Street. Later on he married a Hungarian woman. Once, when he got drunk in the bar, he also showed some regret: "Everyone who we killed deserved it except the two boys!" The bar owner told my father. I knew that he was living near us, but I did not know him, because he worked at the court in Novi Sad and he spent little time in Becse. I knew his wife; she was always looking out of the window.

Once, in the mid sixties when my sister and I went to the artesian well for some water. A Serbian man said that he was very much distressed. He asked us whose children we are and how old. My sister a university student then, spoke to him and I was still in secondary school. He was surprised at our ages and talked to us in a very quiet voice. He asked "Aren't you grown up yet?" He asked my sister to visit him at the Court in Novi Sad. He wanted to get a scholarship for her. We didn't visit him.

Returning to the day of the massacre, September 18, 1944, my mother was left alone on the farm. Later one of our neighbors came to see her and stayed with her until the next morning. The news of the tragedy had spread very quickly. Having heard the news, Cseszák came over early in the morning. He cried and said again and again: "They were very good children." Cseszak left for Hungary, from the farm that morning and died there. His son died in Becse a few years ago.

My father was taken to Verbász. September 18 he and another man were told to go home. He had a bad feeling at once; why? His friend's house was blown up and his family died there. My father came from Verbász to Becse by train. He heard on the train about the two boys who had been murdered in Becse the previous night; they were children. As they talked about it more, he started to recognize the place. He asked who they were and was told. They also said that the mother and father-in-law were in the next railway car, so he could go and ask them. My grandparents lived in Szenttamás and had gotten on the train there. My father went to them and they gave the same news. When my father arrived in Becse, he went to purchase two coffins which he took to the farm. There was an air raid alarm during the funeral so the mourners had to take cover somewhere as quickly as they could; they ran in every direction. My mother couldn't go anywhere; she fainted and was left at the grave. Károly and Gyula Kovács are buried near the church in the Central Cemetery. If you stand opposite the church, it is on your right.

This story was written by Teréz Kovács who lived in Hungary from 1986. I was born in 1949.Please let me know about any events organized in the memory of the murdered innocent people. I would like to do something to help."

FROM SZENTFÜLÖP TO THE GAKOVA CAMP

The next tragic story tells of the woes of the innocent Germans of Bácska. Who stayed in Bácska (Vojvodina), after the withdrawal of the German or Hungarian forces, the Germans and Hungarians alike, were totally innocent people. The few war criminals were smart enough to escape in time.

"If you are writing about the massacres in Yugoslavia, I want tell you my story because I could have been a victim of the bloody events. Although this particular tragedy affected Swabians (i.e. Germans) not Hungarians, but in my opinion, their fate also belongs to the real history of the "liberation" of Bácska. You may have heard about it, but in 46 years I have never met anyone who has. No one I've told about it would believe me or they thought that I was exaggerating. My husband, a reservist, served in the army several times in the fifties. On these occasions, he was usually questioned about his relatives. When answering, he also talked about my relatives and parents. Once he told the real story. Despite the opposition between Tito's regime and our party and government, he was told off in a very rude way: "Don't keep talking about that! It's not true, it's a big lie! The Yugoslavian comrades never committed those crimes!" That's the reason I'm writing about the history of my family and village from the fall of 1944 to the spring of 1946.

Our family lived in Szentfülöp in the county of Hódság in Bácska. Szentfülöp was a village of 5000 people. Its name was Filipovo during the Serbian regime and presently it is called Grasac. Szentfülöp was an ancient village in the early Middle Ages but Turkish troops destroyed the whole countryside. Maria Theresa settled mostly Bavarian Germans here. As I remember, only German speaking people were living here when I was a child.

By the fall of 1944, many families which were compromised had fled along with a number of Volksbundists (German ethnic organisation led by Nazis).

As far as I can remember, the new Serbian regime commenced on November 25, 1944. (This was the date of the liberation.) It was announced that all men over 18 and under 60 had to gather on the church square. Homes were searched by the soldiers. In the afternoon during the shouting and shooting, the women and children were sent back to their houses. They were also prohibited to look out of the windows onto the street. Standing behind the shutters, we saw that the men were leaving the village accompanied by the soldiers. I saw my father and several other relatives among them It was the last time we ever saw them.

We had no news from them for several weeks and every one of us guessed that there was something wrong. The news spread that they had been taken away for forced labor. A heap of spades, picks and shovels were taken after them in carts. It was also said that they had been herded into cattle cars and that the whole group had been taken away to the USSR.

Meanwhile, it turned out that some people had been released. I knew a young man who was among those captured and who was released because his name was Serbian. As far as I remember, he was called Jurisics. I talked to him, but he couldn't or wouldn't tell me anything about the others. I felt that he knew a lot more than he let on. The village priest was also released.

Rumors began to become more and more widespread that a big pit had been dug in a field, into which the men had been shot . There was a farm not far from there where firing and cries could be heard all night. A few years later, I learned that there had been a man who had managed to escape in the darkness and who had been a witness of the whole massacre. He said that the lucky ones had been shot, while the rest had been put to death by means of bayonets and cudgels. We didn't know for a long time how many people had been killed there.

In West Germany organizations, action groups were formed in relation to this affair, one of which was called the Association of the Survivors of Szentfülöp. They organized meetings and also issued a number of publications. According to them, 212 men were killed there that night.

The place of the massacre was surrounded by soldiers. The villagers were not allowed anywhere near. But this wasn't the end of the suffering of the people of Szentfülöp. In the next few weeks, Serbian families were settled into almost every house. They came from somewhere, probably the hills of Bosnia or Montenegro.

The spring of 1945 on Easter Saturday, when there were only old men, women and children left in the village, it was announced that all Swabs had to pack up their things. After the villagers had been gathered together, the march commenced to the railway station where they spent the night. Next day after "mustering", all the packages and personal items were taken away from the poor people. Special care was taken to collect jewelry. People were told that if they couldn't pull the rings from their fingers, they would be cut off. Then they were brutally and cruelly herded into wagons and transferred to Gakova. There were several thousand Swabs huddled together in the sheds and barns or empty apartments under close and armed confinement. I wasn't there at this time only my mother and 11-year old sister. I had been transported for agricultural work, despite the fact that I was only 14. We were also well guarded. The fellows and I harvested the corn first. It was very cold, the work had been left unfinished that fall. It was only after a number of weeks, that I came to the camp of Gakova.

As far as we knew, there were about 15,000-20,000 of us in Gakova. We were sleeping on our sides, because there was very little room. When more and more people began to die, there were more and more free places. Sometimes we had nothing to eat at all. Many starved to death, and others were frozen, but as I remember, many died of typhoid fever. Almost every one was ill.

The attitude of the guards was really cruel and they showed horrifying examples every once in a while to impress their power over us so that we would live in fear. One family made an attempt to escape, but they were caught. They had to carry a board around the camp saying: "This will happen to you if you try to escape." They made them dig their own graves, shot and pushed them into the graves with the whole camp watching. Physical abuse was frequent also. Though they didn't hit me or my sister, they once beat up my mother when she was sent to pick apples with other adults and she tried to hide some for her children.

The number of the dead was increasing all the time. First the corpses were buried separately, in fact they even made coffins for the very first ones. Later on they threw them all in one big pit.

My mother died on January 4, 1946. When it happened, my sister was mostly unconscious with fever and I couldn't go to the funeral either, because I was so ill myself that I couldn't even stand up. Through the window I could see them taking her to the cemetery: many were placed into the same grave that day.

In the spring of 1946, the guarding of the camp was not as strict as before. We even heard of successful escapes. People were fleeing to Hungary, because Gakova was only seven miles from the Hungarian border. A young man who managed to cross the border, after a successful escape from the camp, met one of my uncles who was living in Kalocsa. He told my uncle that my sister and I were alive. He managed to persuade the man to return secretly to the camp and rescue his us; this brave young man took the risk. One night my Sister and I managed to get out of the camp with him and cross the fields to Hungary; it was cold and foggy. It was quite dangerous, because we could hardly walk, and I was coughing and could be heard a distance.

Uncle was waiting for us with a wagon at the border. The rest of the way to Kalocsa was much easier.

We were surprised to see that life in Hungary was about the same. Students went to school, and farmers started working in the fields. There was going to be a wedding at one of my relatives. They didn't know that a few miles away from their home, corpses were thrown into pits by the dozen.

In the massacre of November 25, 1944, my father and four brothers died. In the camp of Gakova my mother, two of my grandparents, an aunt, a niece and her three daughters died; these were my close relatives. Ten to fifteen thousand people died in Gakova.

If the Serbian "heroes" who ordered or committed these terrible massacres are still alive, they probably have high retirement pensions and a lot of medals and badges on their chest.

I've heard about a book published in Germany by *Wendelin Gruber; "In den Fangen des Roten Drachen ("In the Claws of the Red Dragon", Miriam Verlag, Munich)*. I haven't read it, but I know that the details are more exact in this book. The author talked to many eye witnesses; listened to them carefully, and spent a lot of time writing the book.

I don't know how long the camp in Gakova stayed open after our escape. It was obvious that the purpose was to kill as many people as possible and in not to provide communal work. I saw a man in a white coat who may have been a physician, but he didn't take care of us nor give us medicine.

The Serbians solved the ethnic question once and for all over that one and a half year period. On a tourist trip in 1968 we travelled through Szentfülöp and saw the town mayor whose chest was fully decorated with medals. It were obvious that the village was very poor. Before the massacres the village had been prosperous and tidy, with hard working people. The villagers from this earlier period could not be found. The yards were without flowers, a lot of weeds; unpainted and shaky fences, unpainted houses with broken windows. The newcomers didn't feel that it was their village.

Every vault in the cemetery was destroyed. We found the top of our family tomb half pulled away. We could see the bottom of the vault, where there were bones and pieces of coffins everywhere. The marble stones beside the tombs with inscriptions on them had been taken away. Ours were there, but in broken pieces on the ground; we were able to read the lines on the marble. The newcomers' burial places provided the greatest possible contrast; every tomb had its own marble headstone.

Dear sir;
This letter became a very long one. I had never told this story from beginning to end, not even to my grandchildren.
Yours Sincerely,
a Bavarian-Swabian "girl" who feels she has a Hungarian heart."

TEMERIN

"I deserted the Hungarian army. In October there was still a German Tiger tank in front of our house. When the Germans left, an executive committee was formed. We gathered in old Kalmár's Restaurant. In a day or two the Partisan Punitive Company arrived in the village. We thought we were going to be punished, because we had not hindered the deportation of Jews that summer.

A decree was issued ordering all the men between sixteen and sixty to go to the churchyard with a shovel and sandwiches for a day.

The commander knew Hungarian; he said he lived in Zenta.

There was a short man from Ada and a Jew in police uniform among the partisan troops.

The men reported to the churchyard and were ordered to line up. An officer of the partisans stood in front of them with a list in his hand. He had a machine gun on his shoulder and a partisan cap with a red star on his head.

The armed Partisans arrived in four or five horsedrawn carts from Novi Sad, all of them armed. There were no women among them. Everyone obeyed the call, since the Partisans said that whoever was found at home would be shot. Those who had carts and horses had to take them, but they all had to get off and join the others in the line, except for the few who had to carry firewood to the parish hall.

We thought we would have to join the army, but those who were called forth by the partisan officer had to go to the convent. Our line stood between the church and the convent. I became suspicious when one of the guards said to a man whose name was called, "Pass me the shovel, you won't need it any more."

I didn't know any of the partisans. The commander made it clear they had come to collect the guilty, while the rest would go to work. They did not say that they were looking for the names of those who had participated in the raids in Csurog or Zsablya. They didn't care that the person had left the village; they gathered their namesakes in the convent.

They also tried to find the police officer of Nagyada, but out of fear he had hidden in a stack of straw and cut his throat with a razor. His relatives who had to pay the price for him.

Józsi, the leader of our committee had arranged a dinner with the commander early that morning, but when he entered the convent, he came out crying laudly about that he would not take these bloodstained partisans to dinner, after seeing bloody corpses and villagers writhing in agony.

Many were taken to the graveyard to dig graves. In the convent, the Partisans burnt the suspects with cigarette butts to make them confess they had been in Csurog and Zsablya. They were beaten to death even if they did not admit to anything. Someone was beaten to death in the parish hall for not being willing to spit at the Hungarian flag. Those who were not killed in the convent were driven to the cemetery in pairs.

Those who were beaten to death in the village were loaded on a cart by András Komenda, this drove him mad. By the time the procession reached the cemetery, the machine guns had been set up facing the victims. Everybody had to undress and then they opened fire. The town crier ducked into the pit in time unhurt, and later pushed his way through the corpses and went home. His wife kept him hiding in the attic for a long time. When he finally appeared, the "resurrected" was summoned to the village hall and was given a job there."

Horváth the town crier told Sándor Illés, who included this incident in one of his writings. Horváth was exasperated. The town crier bears a grudge against Sándor Illés, because he asked the writer not to mention his name in his writing. It still appeared in Illés's book **"Lament"** along with the story of his escape, and his indignant Serbian adversaries spread excrement on his walls.

Sándor Illés's account of Temerin in **Lament** can be regarded as a documentary source, since the village was his home. Now that Horváth is dead his name and case can be made public.

Several of the partisans from Csurog and Zsablya were responsible for the slaughter in Temerin. They wore civilian clothes and had moustaches. They came . It was they who did the bloodiest "work" in the convent building and at the Scale House.

It was they who drove hundreds of Temerin people to the

Danube bank at Novi Sad to do away with them since they considered the common grave dug at Temerin not sufficiently large enough.

"It was late night when they reached Novi Sad; the streets were quiet, as if the town was deserted. They turn in the direction of the Liman, the Danube bank. Will the terrible massacre of Novi Sad be repeated? Will they take revenge? These simple good peasants had nothing to do with Novi Sad. "Everybody turn to face the Danube", the order was passed by word of mouth. When they turned towards the Danube, the men heard a machine gun being set up behind them. There were several hundred men waiting for death

They were made to throw their belongings from their pockets on the ground. There were lighters, pocket knives,wallets.

There was complete silence except for the rolling Danube River; the trobbing of our heart, and the loud sobbing of one of the men. We could feel rather than see the tall tower of the medieval fort Pétervárad with the bastions and high walls.

As we waited, instead of the machine gun, the noise of a car motor and slamming of the door broke the ghastly silence. Someone started running toward the Partisans, they could hear his shouting in Russian: "Who is the commander?"

The armed civilian reported to the major. "What unit; what company?" the major asked. No unit and no company. He was from Zsablya and had brought the Hungarians from Temerin. "Why did you bring them? What do you want to do with them? "I lined them up for execution; they are Fascist Hungarians." "Let me see the sentence. Show me their sentences of death.", the Russian shouted sharply. Then he tore the gun out of the civilian's hand with a single movement and sent for the commander of the partisans. He arrived and fell into a violent rage, "Private action! Shameful gang! Who are your companions?" The Serb said they had stayed in Temerin. They'll settle the others there." "Arrest all of them.", the partisan captain ordered. "You take these people over," he said to his troops," and make a list of them. No one can lay a finger on them. So to Temerin for the rest of them."

These memories were passed down to the writer, Sándor Illés from his father. What concerns the arrests in Zsablya, and the ban on "laying so much as a finger on the Hungarians," was the creation of old András Illés's conciliatory memory.

The remaining hundreds of Temerin people not yet exterminated by the commandos from Csurog and Zsablya, were ultimately carried away by the partisan commander despite all his "merciful inclinations". The group of several hundred people was then forced to work at the rebuilding of the railroad at Ingyija on the right bank of the Danube. Executions came later, a few at a time, mainly on the elderly.

No one has counted yet how many were executed on the spot and how many died out of the hundreds that were driven away.

The location, size and numbers in the various mass graves is uncertain. The survivors laid a concrete frame over the largest that could be located with certainty, but according to reliable eye-witnesses this frame only comprises the lesser part of the actual huge pit of corpse. Those who still wanted to erect markers or monuments over the greaves were hindered by the Temerin authorities in their reverent intention until the last few weeks.

There was so much blood that flowed from the bodies of men driven out of the Scale House to the market place, that the appointed hearse drivers gathered the rivulets trickling towards the cesspool by the barrel. The ditch, which carried the blood of the dying Temerin men to the market, was dug by careful predecessors to carry the urine of the animals to be weighed. About eight to ten corpse were thrown on each cart, some with their legs hanging out. Some of the bodies were carried to the cart with their trousers down to the ankles and their penises cut off by the murderers. The hearse drivers could not give any reason for the exceptional cruelty.

In Temerin, many can remember the three Hungarians from the Air Force who, were attracted by the girls they met earlier. They hid in Temerin instead of marching away with their unit from Novi Sad in September. They were waiting for the appropriate time to marry their fiances. It was angry partisan women who executed the three fine young men in the cemetery.

The following report was written by the brother of Corporal József Fogarasi, Royal Hungarian Air Force, who was murdered in the Temerin Church Yard: He was stripped, then made to dig his own grave, then machine gunned into a common grave with their hands wired together.It was lucky for the unknown murderers, since the people would have torn them to pieces.

Nationality of the sadist partisan murderers was unknown; they lacked any trace of humanity.

Nationality of murderers: Unknown sadists lacking any trace of humanity called; partisans."

The brother got the information from the female teacher trainee who was bound to József by affections of premarital tenderness.

We are not authorized to mention the name of the girl, a woman over sixty and most probably married.

Temerin is a Roman Catholic village. Religion holds importance and special significance is attributed to the sacraments from Baptism to Extreme Unction, the sacrament of the dead.

Father Koppány and his two curates left Temerin in the fall of 1944, but the parish was not left without a priest after all. The Rev. József Tóth was deposited in Temerin by the last train that left from Novi Sad, and he provided the spiritual needs of the parishioners. He was not harmed and was allowed to hear the confession of the people taken to the convent and intended for execution. He was not given the opportunity to administer Extreme Unction, as it would have been his intention. The number of the mass graves and corpse lying in Temerin has not been ascertained.No accurate data is known about the number of those who were driven away and died. After several months, a man walked down a street in Temerin children, who had not seen an adult man for a long time, pointed at him saying,"Look! A man!".

According to the church registry, a source we believe to be reliable, the total loss of Temerin was 480 people in the fall of 1944.

HORGOS

The reentry of Hungarian troops was not approved by the Dobrovoljacs, therefore twenty-two of them died April 1941 in the ensuing battle for the town..

On October 10, 1944 the partisans arrived, and sacked the church, the convent and the parsonage in the first few days. The parish priest, István Virágh, was not arrested then. Some of the Serbian settlers from Montenegro, who had just returned, remembered that the eighty-one year old parson celebrated Mass in the camp of the Hungarian troops stationed in Horgos. In his sermon, he gave great thanks to the Lord, "God of the Hungarians", for the end of the rule of the barbarians. The 84 year old priest had to be arrested, but there was much debate about what to do with him beyond the usual tortures of captivity. About sixty people, including women, were collected to be victims of the vengeance. István Virágh was still able to celebrate Mass on November 10th.

The bloody day of collective punishment dawned on Horgos on November 20th. The captives were forced to go seven kilometers on the international highway. The sick parson was allegedly tied to a woman. The captives were made to dig their own graves by the road. The Priest was granted the favor of being allowed to watch the grave diggers' work, while he was disgracefully tied up. Then they were slaughtered by their guards.

Legend has it that when István Virágh collapsed, there appeared a bright cross above his figure, and he disappeared in its glow.

This vision was spread by the peasants, who were brought there from the nearby farms to drag the sixty corpses, some of whom they knew well, to the much too shallow grave and bury them.

The corpses were covered by a thin layer of soil. Within a few days arms and legs appeared out of the shallow grave, where stray dogs began to dig up the already decomposing bodies. The taciturn inhabitants of the pit had to be moved to another mass grave. The mass grave was found in 1964, when the former sheepshed was turned into an inn. The mass grave was revealed during the excavation for the drain pipe. The nature of the grave was proved by the fact that there was black cassock fabric among the rags that were unearthed, along with buckles, belts, and other personal objects and bones.

They say that the members of the firing squad were punished by God; they died hideous deaths. The leader of the squad hanged himself in the woods of Szellevény following the murders. Some of the other murderers died of cancer or ulcerous diseases, and most of them committed suicide.

MARTONOS

The Red Army occupied Martonos on October 8th. October 11, the local Serbs had organized themselves and worked up enough courage to ravage the Roman Catholic parsonage, ruin the archives, and the library. They could not have had a reason for bearing grudge against the Roman Catholic Church except for simple religious aversion. They smashed most of the furniture and broke the till open, and took 17,840 pengő cash; a third of the total expense of the church of Kispiac, that was being built. They also dragged the Rev. Mihály Werner along with 23 other villagers.

On November 21, 1944, after more than a month of continuous torture, the priest and his fellow sufferers were loaded on a truck at night and taken to the trenches by the Tisza River, although they had not done anything to qualify them for capital punishment. There had been no atrocity committed in the village against the Serbs in 1941. The majority of the arrested people were perfectly innocent, altough some of them offended Serbs in 1941, but in no way to the extent that would have called for death.

Let us consider the case of Ferenc Holló for an example. When the last German soldier had left the village, Holló, standing in his yard, remarked to his wife, "They won't come back, will they?" This was overheard by his Serbian neighbor, who denounced him for waiting for the Germans to come back. This is why he was arrested and executed.

The tailor Károly Józsa was, at the instigation of a rival Serbian tailor named Congradas Dusko, charged with making a suit for the village notary, Mátyás Fehér, and was finally slaughtered for it. Policeman János Varkulya was executed because he had given warning to a Serb for illegally driving a wheelbarrow on the sidewalk. The same was the case with Ferenc Fejes, Gergely Horváth, János Kéri and Antal Szabó, who joined the police department to support their families. They were of a gentle nature, who did not harm anyone.

Some of the captives were not hurt, while others were terribly tortured. The Rev. Mihály Werner whose genitals were lacerated with pliers day by day by immature Serbian youngsters .

Policeman Sándor Sörös' skin was torn with the bead of a gun. He was skinned alive so that he could not even walk and had to be carried to the execution on a stretcher. The captives were informed by some more humane Serbs that they were to be executed that night, as there had arrived at the village a partisan commando to cover the executions. Mihály Werner, titular Abbot granted absolution to the men in extreme peril. Antal Lendvai confirmed atheist, would not accept the absolution but abused the priest.

Péter Sáfrány, a farmer who had formerly been mayor of the village, knew himself to be guiltless. Nevertheless, he took leave of his wife Klára Csonka; harnessed their two horses; stashed food for a couple of weeks on the cart; and joined the line of fugitives on October 5. He was warned by his Serbian friends from Martonos. He returned from the Transdanubia at the end of April, when the foam of revenge had evaporated. No harm was done to the former mayor except for a few summons.

The massacre of the Hungarians of Martonos originated with Zivojin Putnik, Mita Grubanov, Duric Beljin, Ljubomir Congradac, a butcher called Milo and others. It was carried out by Dusko Petric, Svetozar Bajic and his son Miles, Vlajko Kretin, Dragomir Kojic and a number of young people. One of them had a heart attack, because of the dreadful sight of the execution. Some of the slaughtered were not killed immediately by the bullets, and tearfully begged their executors to kill them and not to bury them alive. This massacre was evidently a war crime like the ones at Adorján, Temerin, Mohol and Bezdán, although neither the originators nor the executors were called to account for the murders.

Some irresponsible Serbian elements planned a large scale massacre at Martonos too, since they considered the 24 dead to be insufficient. The male population was forced to go and work at the ferry crossing on the Tisza, so that after completing a certain amount of work they could be shot into the river.

There were some Russian soldiers at the crossing also. Laskovicz, one of the Martonos residents was ordered there. He had been a prisoner of war in the Soviet Union during World War I, and came back with a good command of Russian. He started talking with the commanding officer of the Russians. The officer asked him why the Hungarians working in front of his eyes were so downhearted and sad. The man said that his fellow workers believed, and not without any grounds, that their guards planned to machine-gun them into the river as soon as the work was finished.

At first, the Russian officer would not believe this explanation for the sadness. Talking with armed Serbians later, he understood that the fear of the Hungarians was not groundless. He then ordered the leader of the Serbians not to do any harm to the Hungarians of Martonos. He obliged the Serbian nachalnik (commander) to report to him concerning the safe arrival of the Hungarians to their homes or else he himself would be shot.

Thus, the mass massacre did not happen at Martonos after the small scale butchery. This is the list of the 24 martyrs of Martonos:

1. Ferenc Bárány, farmer
2. Ferenc Fejős, policeman
3. Lajos Forró, butcher
4. János Gruik, police sergeant
5. Ferenc Holló, joiner
6. Gergely Horváth, policeman
7. Miklós Horváth, agricultural worker
8. Károly Józsa, tailor
9. János Kéri, policeman
10. István Koncz, agricultural worker
11. Antal Lendvai, worker
12. Gábor Nagy, village cashier
13. Péter Ozsvár, worker
14. János Püspök, farmer
15. Kálmán Sáfrány, policeman
16. János Sörös, village mayor
17. Sándor Sörös, policeman
18. Antal Szabó, policeman
19. Péter Szarapka, farmer
20. László Takács, basket-weaver
21. István Török, farmer
22. János Török, fisherman
23. János Varkulya, policeman
24. Mihály Werner, Titular Abbot

ZENTA

After 1919, new rows of houses were built behind the outer row of houses and the cemetery. 2000 Serbian settlers came to live here the "Dobrovoljacs" (in direct violation of the Trianon Peace Treaty, of 1920, which forbade the mass-transfer of population from other territories). By 1941, many of them had learned Hungarian. In 1941, when the Hungarians marched in, some of the Dobrovoljacs thought they would have to defend Yugoslavia in this part of the town. Fifty-two of them paid with their lives for their inopportune assessment of the situation (Serbian data from 1946.)

Nándor Burány, a Zenta born writer, gives the following account in his book **"Collapse"** of the days and weeks when partisan units occupied the town in the wake of the Red Army:

"Now that's exactly what we needed most," the people kept saying, referring to the events in 1941. "It would have been better, if they had not come at all; we used to get on so well. Revenge frightens the innocent as well; revenge is not choosy about its victims...

On October 8th, not more than two hours could have passed when they saw the Soviet troops coming from the river and heading towards the opposite border of the town. Words get stuck in the mouth, perhaps the breath does too.They were walking in small groups or in twos with machine guns on their shoulders. They looked mild-tempered. There was a a reassuring sight, as if they were at home. A bunch of people went to the ferry to meet them with flowers...The first impressions were extremely pleasant. There is no truth in the propaganda spread about the Red Army; the air of hope infiltrated the tense atmosphere.

In the morning, the rumors spread about whose homes were broken into, and whose wife was raped. Pointing a gun at the man, they threw the women on the ground, and laid in the clean beds with their muddy boots on. They took the linen, the clocks, and the better horses from the carriage. Your father carefully smooted away the ruts at the main gate...

The prison under the town hall was filled with "war criminals" . One of your uncles from Tompa was in the prison. You took him lunch. The wife and fifteen year old daughter of a runaway murderer were summoned by the authorities, they were questioned a couple of times, then both of them hanged themselves ... One day the lunch was sent back. The prison was empty and the captives have disappeared.

Later you learn that your relative is all alive and asks you to go on bringing lunch. He and two other persons stayed alive by accident. It was a dreadful night. From the cellar they were led up to the office, were they were registered. They awere undressed and beaten relentlessly, with their hands tied at the back with wire, and they were bound to each other. Rumor has it that the town crier and the notary were the most ferocious...Three prisoners from Tompa side by side. One felt the pliers cutting the wire off his hands. The drunken guards did not notice it. They were thrown out on the pitch dark street. They unbinded each other, and three men run naked in the blind night in the sleet covered street. One run to his friend's houss, covered himself with rags, then climbs over fences, and hides in a hen-house until morning comes. He was nearly frozen to death when he called at the house. They go and get a policeman...

A few months later. Soldiers, prisoners of war and civilians were working on a railway causeway north of the town leading up to the bridge.

They were building a pontoon bridge and a lower causeway leading to it. There is a trench stretching north of the bridge, that was dug by Leventes, when they were expecting to defend the town. The bridge builders are struck by the terrible suspicion that there are corpses lying here, "the hand of one, the foot of the other was left uncovered when the trench was filled up". (*Nándor Burány : "Collapse", Novi Sad, Forum 1968, p 135*)

Burány's text needs elaboration at only two points. The first is the fact that at the flowery reception at the ferry, the Russian officer who took the bunch of flowers from the charming girl speaking Serbian, managed, with the same light movement, to unbuckle the watch on her wrist.

The second amendment: the 64 arrested and tortured captives, were escorted to the pier of the bridge on the dawn of November 10th. Several were shot into the river, and perhaps half of them got stuck under the bridge and were then buried in the trenches.

The 8th Partisan Shock Brigade of Vojvodina arrived at Zenta before the military administration. They declared that the Germans had to be expelled. It is not possible to live in the same country with the Germans after their crimes. The issue of the Hungarians was not yet decided. The same stand, as with the Germans, is likely to be taken again: Thus Hungarians cannot be members of the National Committee for People's Liberation (NCPL); the public use of the Hungarian language is declared prohibited; and the issue of deporting Hungarians is raised.

About a hundred people were arrested as war-criminals. If there happened to be a brave, influential man not restricted in his movement who could vouch for a captive or two, they could be freed.

On November 9, a summary court consisting mostly of self-appointed members, sentenced 64 residents of Zenta to death.

A unit of soldiers arrived from Becse that day by order of OZNA, led by Petar Relic to carry out the executions according to

97

the summary sentences. It is likely that some members of the local militia joined the firing squad, and they may have known their victims.

K. S., eyewitness from Zenta: "They were led to the bath-house under the bridge. Knee-deep in the water, they were mowed down by machine-gun fire. They kept on firing until no one moved."

It was by accident that the illegal court which judged the so called war criminals, left a document detailing its blood thirsty decision. The unorganized shelves of the archives contain the deadly way-bill of sixty-five innocent citizens

1 Mátyás Für, Zenta, 59 years
2 Imre Szabó, Zenta, 1913
3 Péter Dudás, Zenta, 1889
4 István Kovács, Zenta, 1900
5 Ernő Ilovszki, Zenta, 1911
6 Dr Lajos Sas, Csóka, 1910
7 András Czeles, Zenta, 1905
8 Albert Döme, Zenta, 1910
9 Gábor Hagymás, Zenta, 1880
10 Aladár Janek, Obecse, 1911
11 Sándor Guelmino, Zenta, 1890
12 Dr Antal Ferenci, Zenta, 1882
13 Kálmán Johanis, Zenta, 1905
14 Sándor Kesérling, Módos, 1897
15 István Polyákovics, Zenta, 1886
16 Károly Lukács, Zenta, 1915
17 Sándor Halász, Zenta, 1892
18 Mária Puskás, Zenta, 1900
19 Kálmán Hangya, Zenta, 1872
20 Pál Boka, Zenta, 1897
21 Lajos Vecseri, Zenta, 1902
22 István Baráti, Zenta, 1900
23 Tamás Döme, Zenta, 1904
24 János Nagy, Zenta, 1901
25 István Piszár, Zenta, 1915
26 Illés Varga, Zenta, 1899
27 János Bokros, Zenta, 1903
28 Pál Berkes, Zenta, 1899
29 István Kuklis, Zenta, 1908
30 Péter Kovács, Zenta, 1891

31 Dr András Felsőhegyi, Zenta, 1886
32 Dr Károly Balogh, Zenta, 1880
33 József Hesz, Csantavér, 1890
34 György Mihalesz, Zenta, 1906
35 Miklós Tóth, Zenta, 1881
36 Mihály Tóth, Zenta, 1872
37 Mihtly T¢th, Jr, Zenta, 1910
38 Illés Nagy Pörge, Zenta, 1886
39 János Toldi, Zenta, 1898
40 Bálint Huszár, Zenta, 1886
41 Nándor Vass, Zenta, 1892
42 Illés Tóth Katona, Zenta, 1884
43 Marton Franja, Zenta, 1905
44 Jenő Sándor, Zenta, 1886
45 Jenő Halász, Zenta, 1912
46 Gusztáv Lakatos, Zenta, 1910
47 Elek Motynek, Zenta, 1910
48 Péter Tóth Szegedi, Zenta, 1914
49 Lénárd Sic, Rumania, 1902
50 Károly Hadvány, Zenta, 1883
51 Ferenc Imre, Szeged, 1909
52 Géza Boros, Zenta, 1915
53 István Nagyabonyi, Zenta, 1906
54 Gábor Béla Molnár, Zenta, 1900
55 Vasiliye Meskanov, Harkov, 1898
56 Pál Zsiga, Zenta, 1896
57 János Magyar, Hódmezővásárhely, 1912
58 Lajos Bencsik, Zenta, 1904
59 István Kalámár, Zenta, 1890
60 Pál Vass, Zenta, 1896
61 Imre Lálics, Zenta, 1890
62 Vince Lakatos, Zenta, 1908
63 Péter Piszár, Zenta, 1903
64 Jtnos Szollár, Zenta, 1899
65 Lukács Dukai, Zenta, 1883

Members of the committee of war crimes and criminals:(signed) Aleksander and Dusan Milicev
The following witnessed the signing of the document: (signed) Petar S. Senic L.S. Zenta, NCPL

ADA - THE BRIDGE OF LIFE

After the withdrawal of Hungarian soldiers and gendarmes, the Serbs organized to take revenge in memory of the 17 Serbian snipers who lost their lives in 1941. They pondered whether to take at least ten times as many Hungarian lives. Prior to the arrival of the Russians, sixteen persons were executed from among the captives whose number almost reached two hundred, while the rest were driven to yearn for the other world by simple starvation and unique tortures.

It came to Parson Vince Gere's ears that further lists were compiled by the fanatic Serbs of Ada. The arrival of Russian troops protected the Hungarians from further bloody acts. The Parson even divined a method for preventing any further bloodshed. He noticed that in order to reestablish the lines of communication with Bánát, the Russians wanted to build a permanent bridge over the Tisza near the old bridge which was blown up by Serbian sappers during their withdrawal in the war of 1941.

This withdrawal did not make much sense from a military point of view, since it could not cause any damage or disadvantage to the Hungarian authorities who had no control over Bánát. Thanks to the idea of Parson Vince Gere, the ruins of the bridge proved a great help in those days.

Parson Gere offered the responsible French-speaking Russian General, who was short of material, and workmen, two thousand Hungarians from Ada. These men would build a more reliable bridge than that made of pontoons that would survive even a possible ice drift, provided the Russian command guaranteed the lives and possessions of the Hungarians of Ada. Fortunately, the Parson could negotiate with the advice of three Hungarian engineers who had taken shelter in the village. The Russian commander readily accepted the practical and very inexpensive offer, since all he had to do in return was "simply" block any murderous thoughts in the souls of the newly self appointed proletarian leaders of the Serb populace.By the time the bridge was built (from several rows of logs) and the Russians moved on, milder days had arrived and there was less potential for slaughter.

The prestige and popularity of the Parson was recovered as well.

He had established, during the short Hungarian rule a certain degree of respect in the lower level of society by setting up a soup kitchen under the aegis of the parish of St Theresa. He did not exclude the needy Serbian families from the benefit of a regular meal. The Hungarian population of Ada was saved from mortal danger and potential harassment.

If we consider the Serb Orthodox clergy's deep rooted animosity and hatred of the Hungarian Roman Catholic priests in neighboring villages, the contrast is very clear.

MOHOL - DEATH FOR LAND

The agrarian reform of 1920 greatly decreased the landless populace of several thousand in this small predominantly Hungarian town. The Serbian paupers were all granted land, while only the few Hungarian families that were willing to convert to the Orthodox faith were given the same benefit.

There would have been enough land for the destitute, local Hungarians too, since the authorities organized three farming villages near Mohol for the Serbian settlers from Montenegro or Crna Gora.

When the Hungarian army arrived at Mohol in April 1941, the inhabitants of these three Crna-Gorean "Dobrovoljac" settlements, Nyegoshevo, Miltchevo and Svetitchevo were so far from wanting to shoot at the Hungarian soldiers, that they decorated their lapels with palm size red,white, and green Hungarian rosettes for reasons they deemed appropriate. The Hungarian soldiers returned this amicable and peaceful reception with appropriate friendliness.

A few days later, however, the Hungarian gendarmes who replaced the army and began work were ordered to evacuate the Serbian settlers from their homes, and to put them in a train with their scanty luggage. They had to be sent back to their native land via Topolya.

The Hungarian paupers of Mohol thought the time had come to satisfy their old hunger for land, and quickly occupied the three deserted settlements. They did so partly for the reason that the livestock that had been left behind due to the rush had to be fed and watered.

The Hungarians from Mohol were to face a shocking disappointment a few days later. Under new orders, the gendarmes expelled them from their barely warmed abodes with their usual strictness and firmness and moved them back to their humble hovels at Mohol-Ujtelep. This moving in and out involved much more violence than the removal of the Dobrovoljacs with their Hungarian rosettes. The Hungarian villagers' illegal seizure of land was reversed, because the authorities wanted to make room for the Csángó-Székelys coming from Bukovina, Rumania. Nyegoshevo was then inhabited by Székelys from Istensegits ("God Help"), who christened their village Istenáldása ("God' Blessing"), on account of their old village and the rich soil.

In the course of the next three and a half years, there was much quarreling and violence between the Hungarian poor of Mohol and the Hungarian gendarmerie, or the ruling power in general. As a consequence, when Szálasi's Fascist agitators (called Arrow Cross Men) arrived at Mohol and learned about the pain and the disillusionment of the local poor, they promised them land provided they join the Arrow Cross Party which they called the Hungarian Movement. These destitute people did nothing more than sign up and they thought this was about the same as the former conversion of their countrymen to Orthodoxy.

Were they ever wrong! What in 1944 they were given was not land but death. It was child's play for the local Serbs to get hold of the list of the members of the Arrow Cross Party. Supported by the rage of the returning Dobrovoljacs, they made these ignorant men and their families victims of the revenge for land.

The extermination of Hungarians proceeded in an organized way in October and November 1944. A Brain Trust was formed to search for documents and causes for vengeance. They had meetings and made decisions. There was an executive team of younger and more energetic intellectual and craftsmen organizers, whose hands were not stained with blood. The basic work of collecting, beating and torturing people was left to greedy Serbian looters with base and cruel inclinations.More than eight hundred men were gathered.

The Summary Court worked in the barracks of the fire brigade. The victims were cited, dragged to court and accused of fictitious or real crimes. Those who had a match broken over their head, in imitation of the ancient custom of the breaking of a staff, were sentenced to death. they were taken to School No.3 which served as a kind of death row before execution. Seven hundred and sixty matches were snapped over the head of the poor in the Fire Hall.

It was not only Arrow Cross men who were sentenced to death, but everybody who had an adversary or enemy or whose possessions were coveted by one of the "judges".

The captives had to undergo a long torment before the execution. In the course of the several week long torture, the warders could find time to cut straps from their enemies' backs. Jóska Hambalgó witnessed this bloody, inhumane method of torture. The death sentence was not confined to men; young girls 16-20 received the death sentence if their names were found on the lists. Only the sickest, sexual male deviate could invent the horrors of what these girls were subjected to in their last hours.

A curious, almost incomprehensible decision was born in the head of the judges on one of the days of mass execution; the people under sentence had to be shaved. What was this? Inducement of vain hope in the condemned or a gesture of hygiene for the next world? They gathered all six local barbers with their apprentices, if they still had any, and their tools. These men were lathering and shaving the week old beards all day. Sometimes, in the rush, they cut and caused pain to their free customers before death. While shaving that day, the barbers of Mohol counted more than six hundred men .These newly shaved men were then driven to the Tisza at twilight and were shot into the river. A part of the firing squad felt annihilation was more secure on firm ground. The sand pit of Osztrova seemed appropriate for this.

Burying the corpse also promised less work in the sandy soil. The fact that the river often floods the lower part of the sand pit was not given much attention. Those who were undressed in the deadly procession did not have much chance to escape, but there were two or three young men who, freeing themselves from their bondage, were able to run away nude in the darkness of the night. One of these brave and lucky runaways was József Hambalgó, from whose back three straps were cut. He managed to escape and had someone photograph his slashed back.

There is a common opinion among the surviving Hungarians, that Director Constantin Zaumovic is responsible for forcing and passing the death sentences. Two local attorneys, Premislav Radovic and Karakas, took an active share in these sentences as volunteer judges. They were the ones who again and again decided that the Hungarians should be tortured as long as possible before their execution.

The tragedy of Parson Lajos Varga deserves special remembrance. He was charged, while a match was broken above his head, with greeting the arriving Hungarian troops with flowers, and delivering patriotic speeches at the memorial of the heroic Hungarian soldiers on Hungarian state holidays. Allegedly, the Serbian intelligentsia had to participate in these festivals for their own good in order to preserve their jobs, at least they believed so. Parson Lajos Varga was not interested in politics and was free of any racial discrimination including racism against Serbs. He was arrested and tormented because his Hungarian nationality. Among other tortures, all his twenty nails were ripped off with red-hot pliers.

His mother managed, with the help of an influential Serbian acquaintance, to arrange a meeting with her son in the parsonage before his execution. He took an hour to crawl, supported by other men, from the school to the parsonage, which was otherwise a ten minute walk. He had to go barefoot, since his toes were bleeding. His face and head were black and blue.

After his "trip" to see his mother; the guards trod on Parson Lajos Varga and killed him by ripping his stomach open. His body was carried on a wheelbarrow to the sand pit by other people sentenced to death.

Having received belated instructions to take flight, the Szekelys of Istenáldása set forth. Some of them met their fate on the way, some in the internment camp of Jarek. **There was no one to record their sufferings and their death.**

PÉTERRÉVE

"The partisans arrived in Péterréve at about 10 a.m., an hour after the remnants of the Hungarian troops evacuated the village under heavy enemy fire. This was a Sunday in October 1944, and the following day they began to gather the Hungarians, both men and women. Five or six men who served as policemen during the Hungarian rule; then they started gathering the civilians. My 30 year old brother-in-law, János Vermes, Ferenc Takács, the Roman Catholic Parson, and János Koncsik, ashepherd. There might have been about five hundred of them. A number of them were taken to an unknown place and they were never heard of again. Some 60 or 70 men were shot dead on the bank of the Tisza at night. The corpse were buried in the deserted infantry trenches on the bank. Villagers looking for their kinsmen dug up the bodies, but they could not take them and bury them since the partisans discovered them, so the dead bodies were thrown into the river.

I was present when our Catholic priest was executed, since it had been announced that important decrees would be made public on the main square; attendance was compulsory. Our priest was an MP as well. The execution took place Sunday morning after high mass. Ferenc Takács, our dean , was in a cassock, his hands tied at the back, and escorted by 15 armed partisans. He was led to the acacia tree opposite the church, and was shot dead by five partisans before the whole village. They did not even blindfold him. One of these partisans, named Vlastan, still lives in the village and goes about with the veterinarian, helping him with vaccinations. I know the partisan who went to the priest after the execution and pumped two bullets in his head. His name is Vitamir and he works at the town hall. János Koncsik was also executed on the main square, publicly." (János Molnár, 1928)

"I was living at Péterréve when the Hungarian army evacuated. This was on October 8th or 10th.

The partisans arrested the policemen and the priest first. They arrested István Teleki, former army notary; János Fürtös and his wife; police officer Kálmán Kristóf; Dezső Kelemen, a teacher and former Levente instructor; Dezső Helényi, a butcher and his wife who was in the seventh month of her pregnancy; a farmer called Buzogány; and Péter Becsei and his son. A Person called Tüske was shot in the street. About five hundred Hungarians were taken to the cellar of the gendarmerie barracks, and they all disappeared without a trace.

As a fifteen year old Levente, I was ordered to dig trenches and mounds at the Tisza River in July and August 1944. These were the mounds in which the partisans shot the Hungarians they brought there. Fishermen found a corpse on the bank and recognized it as Dezső Kelemen. I heard András Deli, who lived by the river, say that he had seen the partisans preparing to drown Kálmán Kristóf. He begged on his knees not to be executed in such a way. Out of mercy he was made to stand in the end of a boat and was shot into the Tisza." (István Nagy, 1929, Kevevára)

A Serbian gendarme had been shot in a gun battle by the advancing Hungarian troops in 1941.

The 35 persons apprehended by Hungarian counter-intelligence as communists or suspicious elements had included 21 Hungarians, 9 Serbs, 3 Jews and 2 Slovaks.

The partisans collected about a hundred Hungarian residents of Péterréve at the same time as Father Ferenc Takács was arrested. These people were tormented and tortured in the school building without food or drink for three or four days. Finally they were led to the river and shot dead, some into the water and some into the riverside trenches, that had been dug the previous year by Leventes. The rooms of the school were tidied up. The bloody straw was collected, burnt. With some vicious pedantry, new straw was strewn for the newly arrested innocent Hungarian men, who were tortured till they bled just like their predecessors in suffering and death.

The hatred of the local Serbs set the vengeful partisans against Dr Ferenc Takács, a Catholic priest with strong Hungarian sentiments. He was stripped of his cassock, and exposed to the tortures of sadistic female partisans. These acts were aimed especially at the sex organ of the clergyman who had vowed celibacy. At first they tried pliers, but since they were determined to prolong the torture, they went on to burn Takács's penis from the glands upwards with a piece of iron heated on the forge of the blacksmith nearby.

The Catholics of the village were ordered to go to the church square on November 19, St. Elizabeth's Day. The parson, could hardly drag himself along due to the mutilations and torture he had suffered; He had to be propped up. He was led to the side of the church and shot dead before his parishioner's eyes.

This physical torture contained an element of intolerance and hatred of the "other faith" and revenge for the different rules of the Catholic religion, which does not allow its priests to marry. They condemned to death the person who, in their view, might have regarded himself superior because of his celibacy, not only as a Hungarian but as a priest as well. It is no longer possible to find out how large a share of hatred the fellow Orthodox priest may have had in the tormented death of his fellow clergyman. It can be safely said that he was well informed about the lengthy torture but it awakened not the slightest Christian solidarity in his soul.

The data secretly collected by priests for decades in Backo Petrovo Selo recorded, in 1941, four Serbian casualties caused by the Hungarian army and six other people of Péterréve arrested by the Hungarian counter-intelligence. As opposed to this, approximately six hundred Hungarian villagers are recorded as victims of the Serbian retaliation in Péterréve.

CSUROG: TILL THE LAST HUNGARIAN

"In the fall of 1941, Serbian partisans surprised, ambushed, disarmed and undressed the Hungarian police patrol from Csurog in a corn field. **The two bound men were impaled** on a nearby farm."

On December 14, 1943, the court of the Hungarian Royal General Staff accused Lieutenant-General Feketehalmy-Czeydner and his accomplices of executing 869 Serbian residents of Csurog. The Yugoslavian report which was published in Novi Sad in 1946, and can be regarded as an official Serbian account mentions "only" 756 exterminated persons. It seems the Serbian officials did not consider victims of Jewish origin worth mentioning.

Rumor has it that the Csurog Serbs were the loudest members of the deputation that asked for Tito's consent for the liquidation of the Hungarians of their village. This was a reprisal for the Serbian losses in 1942. They were granted the ultimate permission to carry out this intention.

The invasion of Russian troops and Serbian partisans was celebrated on October 23rd. On that same date, the planned genocide of the Hungarians also began. Grown men were shot dead without discrimination, most often in their homes. They killed people by a blow on the back of the head with a pestle picked up in the kitchen; they saved their bullets. These men were then loaded on carts by Hungarians who were to be executed later and buried in the carrion pit.

There was one kind of distinction made between Hungarians. Those who they thought had something to answer for were annihilated in special ways. As a cruel example, a married couple, who had not let their daughter marry a Serbian youth in 1943, can provide a model. The parents were bound together, fastened to the harness of a team of horses and dragged at a gallop up and down the village until their legs almost worn away to the knee at death.

Those who were not killed on the spot were locked in the storeroom of the Village Hall, in the school across the road, and in the nearby granary. Every night for three or four weeks, people were called one by one from a list, never to come back again. Their bodies were mostly taken to the Tisza or to one of the mass graves at the carrion pit of the village. The mass graves have not been investigated, since there remained no Hungarian population in the village who would be ready to remember and mourn.

About two thousand Hungarians were executed in the village, while the rest, mostly women and children, were taken to a camp in Jarek or to the more distant Gajdobra (in Hungarian Szépliget), an ethnic German village turned into a concentration camp.

Those young people who obeyed the summons, could consider themselves fortunate when they enlisted in the Petőfi Brigade. But later, it occurred to the organizer that the 65 would-be recruits were not worthy of fighting against the German. They also ended up in Gajdobra suffering torments and privation.

Let us take a glance at the black pages of Hungarian history with the help of a letter written by a 53 year old Hungarian physician:

"I was born in 1937 in Csurog and lived there until 1944. I cannot remember the exact dates now, nor have I anyone to ask since my father died ten years ago. Although these tragedies still affect the whole family, we were unable to mention or talk about it until now.

My father's parents were executed in 1944, in their own home in Csurog. Their names were István Balogh and Julianna Péter. The story of their execution could be told by my cousins.

My father's brother, Pál Balogh, was killed brutally. I remember my parents saying that it was announced in the village that the executions would be the following day in front of the Village Hall. The relatives who wanted to watch it could go. The sons of my uncle live in Telecska and have a lot to say about this. My aunt died last year. My mother's brother, István Szerda was also executed brutally. On a cold wintry day in 1944, four or five armed men burst into our house and shouted at my mother (father was not at home, he was a soldier) that we should within three minutes go out to the street. There were four of us children, my brother a babe in arms and I, the oldest was six years old. We were put on cattle-trucks the same night. I can remember a long line of people standing in the street, all of them Hungarians. Then we were transported to the camp in Jarek.

We spent, if I remember correctly, nine months in the camp at Jarek. My mother said more than half of the people died; people dropped like flies. The dead were carried to a carrion pit on a cart. The only food we were given was hominy unsalted. Since there was no soap and water, lice were feeding on us. We survived due to the help of our aunt, who would secretly leave the camp at night to steal some carrots or potatoes from the fields.

When we were able to leave the camp, we looked so bad that those in Auschwitz were fat compared to us. We were skeletons standing there in rags, when we were told we could go anywhere except home. There were already people from the mountains of Montenegro or Bosnia living in our house."

The partisan movement could not be stopped by the early Hungarian military actions. The counter-espionage organisation was still looking for the remaining or, newly infiltrated partisans and their supporters. On one occasion, after a long investigation, the gendarmerie collected about twenty people, including the Orthodox priest, whose son had escaped, after arousing some suspicion. The Serb suspects were sentenced to death by the summary court.

The Roman Catholic Priest, Bálint Dupp, appeared before the court and the firing squad saying that they should not punish the father for his son's behavior, wich would be a fatal personal and political mistake. "If you execute him, let me be executed too, for there has been friendship between us so far, and the survival of Hungarian Catholics is at stake..."

The priest's act caused several hours of confusion within the military justice. There were supporting telephone calls. The Catholic congregation flocked around their priest, and they had the support of the Orthodox population, but it was all in vain. While Dupp was away at the county court in Zsablya for further negotiations and ironed out an agreement with Gyula Hazai, the High Sheriff all twenty convicts were executed in Csurog. It is said that a possible prelude to the Orthodox priest's execution, and a cause of the later vendetta, was the fact that on the Hungarian troops' arrival in 1941, the daughter of the same priest went to the commanding officer, and while greeting him in Hungarian fired at him with a pistol hidden in her bunch of flowers. The brave and fanatical girl was immediately shot dead by the surrounding soldiers.

In mid-October, 1944, when the partisans and the vengeful villagers started butchering Hungarians, the Orthodox Serbs defended the Catholic priest from arrest and death, remembering his behavior two years before. In the second week of the slaughter, the son of the executed Orthodox priest turned up in Csurog as a Major of the partisans. At once he demanded the Catholic priest's arrest.

He convened the Village Committee for the Liberation of the People, and demanded that the priest should be executed as "an eye for an eye". The more decent Serbs defended Dupp almost day and night for two days, saying that he had been the one to fight for their priest two years before. The Major then grew tired of bargaining and the apparently invincible resistance of the locals, with some military help from Novi Sad, captured the priest and had him taken to the regional center. There, due to his connections, he arranged that the priest was declared a war criminal and carried back to Csurog with a death sentence. There the major's partisans executed Bálint Dupp in front of his church, without even blindfolding him.

It was not his congregation who maintained the memory of Bálint Dupp's lamentable death, but some better natured old Orthodox men who were ashamed of the deeds of the Serbian villagers. The partisan commander could not gather any Catholics to watch the sight, since those who were left alive were walking now with scarcely any clothes on to the concentration camp in Jarek to lie starving on the bloody straw swarming with lice, prey to the deadly typhus. There remained only a couple of thousand homeless wretches out of the 3300 Hungarian inhabitants of Csurog. They can no longer be united.

ZSABLYA

It cannot be regarded as a mistake that the Serbian list of casualties issued in 1946, knew about 72 fewer Serbian martyrs than what the Hungarian Generals and Colonels responsible for the bloodshed were accused of by the Hungarian Chief of the General Staff. (The reason for the Hungarian retaliation was the partisan activity originating from the Bánát, which had eleven Hungarian victims: two policemen, seven border guards and two gendarmes.)

The Hungarian court laid charge to 653 Serbian victims, while the Serbian indictment referred to only 581 victims. The extent and ferocity of the retaliation was not diminished by this numerical difference.

The retaliation against the Hungarians started as soon as the Russian troops and the partisans arrived. They began gathering the Hungarians, most of whom were immediately executed on the spot in the most savage and ferocious of ways. Many of the more well-to-do Hungarians, whom the Serbs disliked, were drowned in the filth of the latrine. Others were beaten, whipped to death, and many of the real or iimagined adversaries of the Serbians had their finger nails torn off first. Some victims were dragged to a smithy and burnt with a hot iron. The passion for burning and singeing naked sex organs increased the partisans thirst for inflicting more pain and passing the intervening time by literally destroying the captives piece by piece.

Some of the partisans lost their patience, gave up the pleasures of torture by burning, and flogged the backs of naked Hungarian men until their skin came off in strips. Those who died during torture were buried in the carrion pit.

A father had eight sons executed. The father was killed first, and his sons had to accompany him to the execution in parade step. His youngest son, thirteen years old, refused to march. Though beaten savagely by the murderers, the teenage boy held out and did not do the parade step in spite of the beating. All his brothers were executed one by one. When he was led to his own execution, he spit at his guards, who cruelly knocked out his teeth in turn before killing him.

István Máté, a Store owner (born 1911), who escaped in a miraculous way, recalls those weeks:

"I was living in Zsablya in October, 1944. The partisans invaded the village at 4 p.m.. Péter Fekete, a farm worker with seven children, was caught and hanged on a mulberry tree in front of the Village Hall, and left there for three days to the horror of the public. The partisans wrongfully blamed him for collaborating with the gendarmerie.

I was arrested the same day as Peter Fekete. I was locked up in the village jail. Every day twenty to thirty people were pushed into the room. They were always questioned and tortured at night. Péter Fekete's brother was tortured savagely; he died in jail. He said his brother's testicles had been pulled back with a piece of wire and smashed with a hammer. We took the dead bodies to the cemetery on carts. I had to dig graves, which were 8 meters long, 4 meters wide and more than 2 meters deep. Fourteen cartloads of corpse, that is 150 people, were buried in each of these pits. On the way out, I had to lay on the corpse lest I should get shot. There were thirteen or fourteen year old students among the corpse. The victims were made to undress first and were then executed with machine guns. I recognized András Magyar gendarme, Vida Börcsök inn-keeper, András Csirpák, a disabled soldier, High Sheriff Béla Bukováry, Péter Kutri, József Börcsök and János Börcsök among the corpse; they had all been judges or members of the jury. I know about five mass graves in Zsablya."

The following is an account of Mrs. Teréz Gregus:

"My younger brother, Bandi, was taken away on Sunday and was executed in the yard of the Village Hall. The Feketes were executed at the same time, father and sons, in the order of their ages; János, Sándor, Feri and all the younger ones too. All the male members of the Bun and Gosztonyi family, and old Teca

Hagymás. She had been outspoken all her life, and kept talking back to them insolently:
"Shoot in my ass", she turned her backside towards them; she was shot in the head.
Terus Kelemen and an other woman was also executed then.
Mihály, my husband, managed to hide on the farm. One night he came for me:"Let us flee to Novi Sad". We hid there till spring; this was not without danger. My parents were taken to the Jarek camp in January."

Those few who were left alive were driven to Backi Jarek on January 23, 1945. Their homes and all other properties were confiscated; they could only take their clothes with them. Those who had a horse or a cart were allowed to go to Jarek by cart, but once there, their horses and carts were taken from them. There was much starving and torment in the transit camp too. Many died of hunger, others of epidemics. An old German internee was given the job of picking up the dead every morning with a wheelbarrow. He collected and buried about twenty or thirty dead bodies each day.
The guards were very cruel. In the middle of winter, the internees were forced to walk from Jarek to Gojdobra in the severest cold. One of the women was from Martonos originally, and was moved to Zsablya well after the raid in 1943. Her husband was immediately executed, while she was interned along with her ten month old daughter. They were poorly dressed, she had to walk from Jarek to Gajdobra in the coldest weather. At one point, the baby's scarf fell off her head. The cruel and bloodthirsty partisan who was escorting them did not let the mother pick up the child's scarf, saying, "She does not need it, at least she'll croak sooner".
According to reliable estimates, at least 2000 of the Hungarian population of Zsablya died, most of them were executed in their village, but many died of starvation or contagious diseases in camps.

DEATH OF THE PUNTERS

To the Punter Districts belong, besides the already mentioned Csurog and Zsablya, Sajkásgyörgye (Gyurgyevo). Sajkáslak (Lok), Dunagárdony (Gardinovce), Sajkásszentiván (Sajkos), Tiszakálmánfalva (Budisava), Tündéres (Vilovo), Mozsor

(Mosorin), and the "capital" or "capital village", Titel. These villages have been privileged since the Turks reached the Danube. The Punter Organization was born around the time when the Turks came to our frontiers. After they had been driven away. the Punter Soldiers relocated their quarters for the defence of the frontier Pozsony and Komárom to the Punter District of Titel, functioning up to the end of the 18th century. After the expulsion of the Turks, there was a Serbian majority among the punters. Some of their privileges, which were the pride of the swift boatmen, remained intact.

Puntership is much older than infantry; it preserved far more features of ancient Hungarian warfare. The Danube did not allow the use of large warships. Instead, the small boat (sajka-punt)) was used for defence, transport and even offensive operations during the Turkish wars. The institution, whatever the crew working within it, kept its Hungarian character.

Navigation had demanded special knowledge. It wanted only professional soldiers and professional boatmen. Chiefs had been elected from among the crew. The private soldier, if he distinguished himself, became a corporal and a nobleman. The best corporals then became chieftains.

The treasury paid the Punters by the year. They had a number of privileges. With the advent of modern warfare the importance of the Punter Force disappeared, but the spirit of these fearless fighters of the rivers lived on. This inherited self-confidence has remained prevalent in the neighborhood of Titel up to our time. The Hungarian military authorities, as well as Tito, should have taken this to account in the vendetta, when they roused and unleashed the punters' anger.

Gyurgyevo and the Rusyns

The subsequent investigation by Hungarian military authorities failed to recognize the consequences of the raid affecting Sajkásgyöngye. Whether there were partisans here in 1942, it would be hard to say today. What is certain knowing the nature of the organising methods of the partisans, they could have had supporters. Did they deserve sanctions for that? Maybe. The 1946 report from Novi Sad records two hundred and forty-four Serbian and Rusyn victims. Almost half of the four thousand and five hundred people living there were Rusyns.

The majority of the 300 Hungarians, when sensing the desire for revenge , left Gyurgyevo on the heels of the retreating Hungarian forces.

For lack of Hungarians to take revenge on, the Serbians vented their anger on the Rusyn population. This was due to the fact that, having had no contact with the partisans during the raid, they had hardly suffered any losses.

They had been fair to the Hungarian authorities from the beginning, a fairness which the later returned. The partisans, besides massacring the few Hungarians who did not leave, they behaved as cruelly to the Rusyns as if the later were Hungarians. They executed the headmaster, Marvojlovics, because he spoke Hungarian and supported the idea that besides knowing the conversational language, children in his classes should learn Hungarian. They cruelly tortured the Greek Catholic priest Michael Böszörményi. He was shoed like a horse and driven to Novi Sad barefoot in that pathetic condition, only to be executed after further cruel tortures.

In 1944 several hundred Rusyns fell victim to the partisans in this way as a consequence of the 1942 raid which they had nothing to do with. The reprisal did nor spare those who showed the slightest sympathy with the Hungarians or those who expected the Serbian Royal Government, with its seat in far-off London, to return.

Also doomed to die was an aged woman, Kata Babe, who operated a small boarding house. In 1943, she received an order from a Serbian youth to poison, on "superior orders", the two young instructors staying in her house. He even left some poison with her. These two teachers had gained considerable popularity by their humane methods in the Serbian classes, even with Serbian parents.

Kata Babe accepted the poison but did not put it in their food, because she was fond of them. She was afraid of the consequences and did not want to be a murderer. This lad, now an ardent partisan, personally shot and killed the disobedient Serbian woman.

Sajkáslak

The raid could have spared Lok, but at the end of 1941, a few partisans rowed over the Danube and shot three sentries. It was on Easter Sunday that the Hungarian soldiers executed Serbians said to have sympathized with the partisans. The parish priest desperately tried to explain to the lieutenant lodged at the parish, that the captives still waiting to be executed were innocent. The new group to be executed had just been lined up in front of the firing-line when the parish priest, János Gertner, arrived and prevented the act. The lieutenant was relieved to see that the Hungarian militiamen were glad to put an end to the massacres.

Fifty-three Serbians had to suffer, for the most part innocently, for the " heroic exploit" of the "visiting" partisans.

This is the village where the number of people killed by the partisans remained below that of the victims of the raid. "Altogether" there were twenty-eight innocent Hungarians executed. Those who, under the direction of the militiamen, took part in the massacres of 1942, had fled.

The relatively few captives were not treated very well here, either. Those who did not want to admit even a slight degree of guilt or did not want to deny their nationality, were shot in the mouth or were hanged from the window-knob (strangled by a cord) and were then transported to the knacker's yard.

Most of the inhabitants of Sajka destined for execution in return for the humanity of the Catholic parson were saved by the Orthodox priest. Special gratitude was owed in a matter involving the iconostasis. It had happened that in 1941, the "connoisseurs" among the militiamen took down the icons of the Orthodox church, and with the purpose of enriching the Catholic church, took them to the parish office and handed them over to the curate Fábián Quintus. He, with an inventory, graciously accepted them from the soldiers and when the generous battalion passed on, he took the whole set back to the Orthodox church with apologies. The majority of Hungarians and the Catholic church were then left unharmed.

Nevertheless we cannot forget about the executed victims:

1.Péter Pásztor, forester
2.Antal Csorba, owner of a threshing-machine
3.István Konrát, policeman
4.Sándor Milánovics, pubkeeper
5.Károly Milánovics, Sándor's son
6.János Krizsán, farmer
7.András Krizsán, János's father, farmer
8.Ferenc Varga, farmer
9.István Tokos, shopkeeper
10.István Tokos, the shopkeeper's son
11.György Zorád, owner of a threshing machine
12.Sándor Kiss, policeman
13.Mihály Kormos, fisherman
14.Ferenc Varga II, farmer

15.István Nagy
16.János Paska
17.István Kasza
18.Ferenc Hegedüs, farmer
19.József Halász
2o.János Bagi, policeman
21.Antal Tóth, the first to be shot in the street
22.Sava Radosaljevics and
23.János Kalapáti,Levente-instructors,
24.Antal Dujmovics, policeman
25.Pál Dujmovics, a twelve-year old boy
26.Mihály Ternovác
27.János Bozsó
28.Antal Csuka

From **Dunagárdony** (Gardinovce) and **Sajkásszentiván** (Sajkas) we have no data about the massacre of Hungarians in 1944 of these two sparsely populated settlements. They were practically defenseless and the 1981 census counted seven Hungarians in one village, eighteen in the other. The bloody reprisal was inevitable, because the 1946 registry book records thirty-eight and seventeen Serbians, respectively, who fell victim to the Hungarian raid.

In **Tiszakálmánfalva** (Budisava) the partisans regularly blew up trains. Because of this, the raiding Hungarian Corps rounded up the peasants from the Serbian farms that surrounded the railway. After lining up the first group at the wall of the Village Hall, prepared to execute twenty people. The Hungarians living on these farms, who had been living in peace with their neighbors all along, rushed to the scene and surrounded the victims pleading for their innocence, prevented the reprisal. The militiamen did not shoot.
The partisans entering in the fall of 1944, were not informed of the humanitarian act of the Hungarian peasants. On October 20,they rounded up some thirty of them who never came back. They were said to have been transported to Zsablya and were exterminated.

In **Tündéres** (Vilova) there was no one to protect the Serbians picked out as victims for the raid. The Yugoslavian registers record sixty-three victims. The reprisal of the returning partisans was inevitable and it mostly afflicted the Hungarians who had just come over from the Szerémség. The rest of them were destined to be driven to the Jarek camp in January 1945. Eighty people tried to defend their new houses, where many died on their porches.

The two thousand inhabitants of Titel diminished to one-third of their original number, just because of their native language. Fifty-two Hungarian males from Titel paid for the execution of fifty-two people suspected of being partisans or of being their accomplices.

Mozsor - the Cain-sacrifice of the sinner priest

The geographical features of Mosorin were favorable for large scale partisan activities. The Hungarian frontier guardsmen had to face and reckon with the presense of partisans since the summer of 1941, also in the form of actual combat causing significant losses at times. The raids, lasting for several weeks, often combed the farms on the floodplain of the Tisza hunting for suspects and partisan-accomplices. According to a Yugoslavian publication from Novi Sad one hundred and seventy-nine people from Mosorin were found guilty.

The partisans took revenge on the five hundred Hungarian inhabitants of the village for their own losses. On November 2, 1944, after a series of tortures (tearing off nails, smashing testicles, ripping abdomens) sixty Hungarian males were shot or beaten to death. Some of them were thrown into mass graves, others were tossed into the Tisza river. The ripping-open of abdomens was inflicted on dead bodies as well, so that the water would not cast them bloated, before due time. Those who remained alive were driven, with the exception of two families, to the Jarek Camp with the threat that if they returned they would surely be killed. Only the Jakubetz and the Szekeres families were allowed to stay home. Twenty-one Hungarians were found in the village in 1981.

Special attention should be given to the very sad story of the Catholic priest:

The Rev. István Köves had good reason to escape with the militiamen. The priest, a shame to his brethren, had not been able to resist the temptations of this world for several years. He was generally known for his avarice by his own congregation. He reported rich Serbian and Jewish families to the police, accusing them of seditious crimes. Some members of the accused families were executed, and others were carried off by force. Their valuables, jewels and money, were appropriated by Köves.

The Serbians kept in mind the priests crimes and apart from physical reprisal, they had an eye on the jewels. In a few weeks they managed to detect the fact that István Köves had fled to

Jánoshalma in Hungary. The war and the mobility of the Soviet army still made the borders merely technical. It was not too difficult to send an armed partisan group to the place of refuge. They did not care too much about the lawfulness of the deed, they dragged the priest, together with his midwife-housekeeper and her mother, back to Mozsor. All three of them were tortured to extract from them the hiding place of the jewels. First the midwife, then the priest admitted that the jewels were hoarded in a safe place under the altar.

The church, already desecrated, was completely demolished by the Serbians, and the Roman Catholic cemetery was also destroyed. The Rev. Köves, like St. Lawrence, was burned alive, but without the possibility of future sainthood. At the same time the midwife, raped, was strangled and having deserved a lesser torture her mother was slaughtered too. The number of victims in Mozsor thus rose to seventy-two.

ZOMBOR

In 1941, the Hungarian troops of the Pécs Corps reoccupied Zombor The first night the chetniks, having hidden in the attics, caused long street battles and extensive fires. There must have been forty of them against the garrison of one thousand firing away aimlessly. That day and the following morning the poorly trained and disorganized Hungarian troops made themselves ridiculous, because they were unable to capture, either alive or dead, any of the fighting chetniks. Six Hungarian militiamen died in the street-fighting , sometimes hit by a Hungarian bullet. In the next few months, the Hungarian counter-intelligence found eleven people in Zombor with its Serbian majority, who could be accused of seditious crimes.

Compared to all this, the reprisal initiated by the returning Serbian military authorities was gigantic.

In the last moments of the "Hungarian era" on October 20th, the counter-intelligence happened to find, on the captured Serbian leader, Patarcsics, the black list of those Hungarians of Zombor who were to be executed at the first opportunity by the entering partisan militia. Out of a sense of duty, the counter-intelligence warned those on the list to get away. Most of them left with the last retreating Hungarian troops. Surprisingly, first mentioned on the list were two Carmelite Friars, Gellért Sztancsics and Illés Hollós.Their most serious crime was obviously their patriotic sermons.

Many who did not get notice of their imminent death or simply felt innocent, chose to stay but they "got on the hook" when the Russian and partisan troops entered. Some literally got on the hook; they were hanged.

Rounding up Hungarians destined for death was not confined to the town. The Hungarian males of the surrounding villages were taken to the Kronich Palace by force. From Bezdán, some five hundred men were taken. Here they were beaten all day, and there were some bloodthirsty, sadistic, partisan women who were especially active. In different corners of the apartment halls, their activities were being watched by their fellows with guns pointed, ready to fire if one or another of the tortured men attacked or resisted the strikes of the gun-butts. This would give them sufficient reason for a massacre.

It is from the survivors of Bezdán, that we know of the horrible weeks spent starving, laying on straw full of lice and blood in the Kronich Palace. Here everyone believed themselves condemned to death, as they did not know who would be the next ones to be loaded on trucks heading for the Danube or the Ferenc Canal.

There were also bound prisoners, taken by force to the race track where they found common graves waiting for them. The partisans did rather a rough and ready job on the executions. Not all the victims were hit mortally, these too were rolled into the grave. From beneath the layers of half-buried bodies, one could still hear moaning of the people still alive several hours later. 2,500 people were executed n the Race Course alone

More than once, the tortured ones were forced to run over hot embers barefoot, before being driven in front of the firing-line. It is said that the platform of the recently finished bus terminal is the marker over a huge mass grave. The other "depot", the barracks, was only used as temporary quarters that November. There "only" two hundred people were shot at most.

A young Serbian butcher from Monostorszeg, who was taken into the ranks of the partisans because of his butchering skills, boasted sometime later that he took part in the execution of at least three thousand people.

According to some brave parish priests of ours who collected information in the neighborhood of Zombor, 5,650 innocent Hungarians fell victim to the vendetta till the middle of November. Drawing up a final list, if only for their remembrance, seems impossible.

Let us remember one person, however, the Judge István Sugár, who went to buy some bread one day and never returned.

VERBÁSZ

The Hungarians remaining in the richest village of Bácska remember that three hundred and fifty people disappeared from among them. The murderers forced them to dig their mass grave in the cemetery.

There were burials in the vicinity of the hemp-processing factory of Óverbász. To make things easier, the murderers also threw dead bodies and some that were still alive, into wells.

The memory of the Germans who were driven away and executed is fostered by the Hungarians in Verbász.

"Hearing you," a letter reads, "is as if the graves that hide our dead, ages 14-60, were suddenly in front of me. There is one grave in the cemetery of Verbász, where there are one hundred and one bodies. (The list of names can be found in a book published in West Germany.) These are the victims of the notorious investigations of November. They were usually taken away three times; first they were allowed to go home without being in any way injured; the second time they were driven home completely naked; then the third time they were headed for the cemetery.

In 1967, I went to the Cemetery with my family. My aunt only dared to show me the grave with her back to it. In it lay my war-disabled uncle, the headmaster and teachers of the local Hungarian grammar school, and the Germans who had sympathized with the Hungarians and who had stayed behind in their naivete.

In the spring of 1945 came the suffering in the Gajdobra Labor Camp for several months. My aunt was taken there with her four children and also her parents (the Transylvanian writer Károly Molter's brother and niece). Insufficient food, saltless gruel and unripe ears of corn took lives. Only a seven and a one-and-a-half year old child survived it, because they were released at the request of my aunt, whose husband had been killed.

I remember that the local Serbians once sent a petition to my father, he was the local doctor, asking us to stay because life had to go on and they would guarantee our safety. My parents did not want any more of a minority life and decided to leave.

The most horrible things were not done by the inhabitants of the village, but by Tito's partisans with the help of a few local villains. These were: Gyakula Pero, Sijadcki Vlado, and one named Marko who was familiar with the local circumstances.

Please be discreet with these rather personal comments, because one can never be careful enough and I have grandchildren living there and I would like to go home from time to time."

PACSÉR

At Pacsér sixteen Serbians fell in the shootings in 1941. Two hundred Hungarians had to suffer death for it. It was the butcher, Ivo Jovkovics, who organized the administration of "justice" and the death-ceremony on the road leading to Bajmok, where three big mass graves were dug with the help of the Third Battalion of the Eighth Brigade of Vojvodina. They picked a district inhabited by Hungarians and those who were found there were all driven to their graves.

The Rev. József Kovács was seized separately. In the course of an inspection, an officer of the brigade recognized Kovács as an old schoolmate. It was not easy for him to save the priest, as his accuser, since a church going Catholic Serb insisted that the priest was a great enemy of the Serbs. He had often been heard glorifying the Virgin Mary, protector of the Hungarians. The priest, no longer under threat of death, tried to save the villagers already rounded up, but the partisans of the Third Battalion preferred to follow the butcher, Ivo Jovkovics. Even the old schoolmate supported his efforts, but the two hundred Hungarians had to die anyway. On their grave, the dissembling, careful, Serbian generations planted wisteria, to cover the crimes of their fathers.

BAJMOK

The local Hungarian Counter Intelligence Group took thirty-five Serbians to concentration camps, although the burgomaster pleaded their innocence with his peasant naivete.

In the middle of October 1944, the Russian troops occupied Bajmok, and the partisans appeared on their heels with people who had been released from captivity by the Counter Intelligence Agency. They brought with them an ardent desire for action, which was a desire for reprisal. On the first night of their arrival they rounded up seventy-eight Hungarians and two Germans. They tortured them for days at the Village Hall; pretending they were selecting some. One or two friends were saved by some Serbians through a side door of the movie house, where the people to be executed were kept. That is where the Pharmacist, Ernő Jeszenszki, the owner of the pharmacy called "Guardian Angel" was held. He was known for his willingness to help anybody who came for help. Apart from being a Hungarian, he was found guilty of being knighted by Regent Miklós Horthy in 1941 for his heroism in World War I. This was considered by Titoist and Stalinist standards, equal to being a Fascist.

After long tortures, the partisans took their captives to the clay pits near the railway bridge, where they shot their victims by the hundreds. The bloody work was easier since they did not have to dig, just dump soil on the bodies. The owner of the previously mentioned pharmacy was thrown on the heap too.

The males of the village fled to the edge of the village where they spent the night in the cornfield so they would not be found. Those who joined the workers in the field during the day had done so in wain, since the the partisans herded the villagers into the moviehouse, the anteroom of hell, together with their hired workers. The number of victims slowly rose to one hundred and fifty. Later on new pits had to be dug at the railway bridge, the old ones now being full. The newly arrived, foreseeing their destiny in the dead bodies laying there, first covered their fellows with soil, then made room for themselves before they surrendered, half naked, to the machine guns. The inhabitants of the nearby farms had to listen in horror to the constant rattling of guns and the cries "Help, Hungarians!"

The murderers left no burial mound. If there was a mound they stamped it into the ground, singing and dancing triumphantly.

The following spring, when the farmers horses went to plough, they sensed that the field no longer supported life.The horses reared, snorting, when they approached the field. That field, consecrated by Hungarian bodies, remained unplowed due to the homage paid to it by these horses. The people who were left behind kept coming back to pick up a rag, a cap, or a shoe, which were useless to the executioners.

The fate of the Judge Károly Czimbell deserves special notice. We have already mentioned him - anonymously - as one who did his best to save his Serbian fellows. The retreating gendarmes warned him to get away because he would be the number one enemy of the partisans, since he was in a responsible position. He did not ignore the warning, although he believed that he was innocent. He went along in painful march with the gendarmes as far as Baja, but there he got on a cart going to Bajmok and returned to his family after a few days absence. He did not even have time to take a bath before the partisans came to get him. They kept in mind his suspicious though short absence. After a short beating they skinned Czimbell Károly alive before putting him on a truck and throwing him into the mass grave without his skin; he was still breathing.

SZABADKA

The town, which inaugurated its new Major, Andor Rökk, on January 19, 1942, was spared by the raid of the partisan hunters. Serbian data from 1946 says that during the days when the Hungarians came in, one hundred and forty-seven Serbians fell victim to the change of regime in April 1941. They never mentioned the number of Hungarian deaths. The Hungarians of Szabadka had to pay a high price for this in the fall of 1944.

The town was occupied by the Russians and the partisans on October 10. After a few days orientation, they started to round up the Hungarians. At dawn they drove their jeeps to get those who they had singled out. There was always a Russian soldier with them, accompanied by partisans wearing machine guns. To keep things moving along smoothly, they kept saying that the person summoned as a witness at this early hour was to be taken in only to give a statement. These witnesses, who were never interrogated, were either taken to the barracks on Palicsi Street or to the yellow house in Agnes Lane, to the much feared Counter Intelligence Center of the Home Affairs Authorities. After being severely tortured, the only place for them to go was the cemetery.

Here, without any trial, verdict, or even an explanation of any kind they were shot and dumped into the pit. Beyond the seedy buildings of the old hospital (now a factory) on a clearly outlined piece of land, there are three rows of mass graves of twenty by twenty meters each. They must have been dug by those who followed, when the enormous pit was full. The partisans tried to mask the noise of the guns and the death cries by sounding the air raid siren. Without guns, it was impossible for the Hungarians to help their family and friends or fellow Hungarians. The neighborhood counts five mass grave sites.

According to some, there were two thousand Hungarians from Szabadka to have been interred beside the old hospital. According to the Priest as many as seven thousand were slain.

It is generally known in Szabadka that the executions were led by Strazsakovics Blasko. He is responsible for the death of those massacred innocently.

The writer Károly Dudás and the film maker Zoltán Siflis asked Strazsakovics Blasko to be interviewed before a camera. Blasko, to mitigate his past crimes, was willing to show his face and answer questions directly.

Many still believe that he was at the time the military commander in Szabadka, master of life and death. In fact he was the commissar of the police that had just come into being. As a commissar, he was subordinate to the police commander and his deputy. It is true that his word always decided matters.

Eugene Nyárádi the police commander, had a Rusyn conscience despite his Hungarian name. His deputy was Tomilica. As a member of the committee for the liberation of the people, he was charged with the task directly by General Ivan Rukovina and Major Pavle Gerencsevics. Their headquarters were the previously mentioned hated and much feared Yellow House.

Strazsakovics held the OZNA responsible for the unlawful acts. He, the political commissar of the local police said that he was uninformed of the activities of the OZNA. He said that he did not even know the names of the people involved.

Strazsakovics gives the following explanation of his last knowledge of the mass death of the Hungarians:

"One morning I was going to my office, and I heard loud noise in the building. The guard saluted and I asked him why all the noise. He said the arrested people were being noisy. I made him open the door of the hall. As the door opened, the people began to swarm towards me shouting; "Blasko, Blasko, Balázs, help."; all of them wanted to talk to me at once. I knew many of them, and many of them knew me. There and then I let all go free without asking the commanders for permission. Later Eugene Nyárádi came up to me saying, "Blasko, why did you let those people go?" I said to him "They committed no political crime. There was among the released Hungarians Anti Ódor, commander of a Battalion under the Hungarian Commune. in 1919. You were not from here, you can't know these people." He was younger than me, hardly twenty two; I was thirty at the time. "Most these people would have said in 1941 `you bloody Serb` or `stop kidding me you lingo tongue` as some said such things to me too. We were not to deal with such people.

Not much later the town commander, Milos Tadijin, sent for me; he had a colonel called Jovanovics with him. They asked me why I let the enemy go free, when there were some among them who had been bemedaled by the Hungarians in World War I. "What do you want", I said, "you could get such medals for a sip of whisky. My father had a sackful of them up in the attic."

"I must have let about seventy people go. Who rounded up these people? A student called Mile, who arbitrarily named himself police commander of a district. He went from house to house, questioned people, and arrested some. Well, I punished this student.

"Now, about the executions. It happened just before the introduction of the military administration. One night I was going home to my parents' house. It was dark, like inside a sack. When I got to the second district, in front of the church, a truck drove past. The only thing I could make out was that there were people on it. At the corner I also saw that they were accompanied by others wearing guns. As I got home and opened the gate I heard tratratratratra...and I heard the moaning. I was horrified and said to myself, excuse the word, "you mother fuckers, you murderers."

"The following day I met the deputy of the military commander, Matija Poljakovics, and I told him what I had seen. He told me that was the way things are, that there were a lot of people arrested and there still would be."

"Now a few words about how they rounded up the people. There was a Serb here called Franje Pujindzsics, we only called him Farsa. He was a nice, liberal thinking man. He was sincerely happy about the fall of Fascism and the liberation. At the time, I was already the commissar of the military command. Poljakovics was telling me that Farsa's wife was desperately looking for her husband, she wondered if we had sent him somewhere. I made inquiries and sent her to Lajos Jaramazovics, president of the local liberating committee. Jaramazovics came to me with her, said I was on the military staff, but we could get no information. I made inquiries with the officers of OZNA, who I only knew by the names Milos, Uros, Vanja and Csapo. At last Poljakovics got the information that Farsa had information about a Croat. He reported that he hobnobbed too much with the Croatian Fascists. This man reported Farsa, so there would not be any witnesses and Farsa was eliminated".

"I do not know how severe the reprisal was, but I am sorry it happened. I am sorry we did the same as Horthy's Fascists. I am sorry it was a reprisal, although the military court already existed and it should have happened through those channels. Many became victims; there were surely some who were guilty but not so much as to deserve death. Those who survived these first months, later got away with a few months in prison."

"The OZNA kept twenty-five workers here; these were mostly privates from the country. The people from Szabadka knew me and thought that I was fully involved. I only put one person to death, because he had killed and robbed a lonely woman. The victim happened to be a Hungarian the criminal a Serbian. The woman hid this Serbian, who was an army deserter.

"It is not a secret that, behind the cemetery, where the Mackovics brick factory once stood, there is a mass grave. We used to organize sports events there, later it was closed. After the war, Tito visited Szabadka. He gave a long speech here and in the introduction he said something hardly anyone understood; I understood. He said:

"You have done some cleaning up here; now you'll have to go on working."

"I understood that through the OZNA, he had exact information about the nature of the cleaning. If there had been but a few war criminals killed, he would not even have been informed. I can only estimate the proportions the massacre took, and that rather without responsibility, I should say. On the whole territory of Szabadka including the Germans that were executed here when the partisan brigade left, some three hundred and fifty people were executed. To me it is just as much reprehensible as what the Hungarians had done some time before."

Let us add to the statement, which tries to mitigate and deny the responsibility of the officer, the recollections of two young people who managed to survive.

"I passed my final exam in the grammar school of Szabadka in 1942. In my class there were three or four Serbians, three or four Bunjevaces (a small Slavic ethnic group, related to the Serbs) and one or two Jews (Francois Bondy, for example, the literary expert living in Switzerland) besides the Hungarians. Our relationship was characterized by true friendship and by the tolerance characteristic of the people living in Vojvodina. The people who taught Hungarian literature were József Bogner and László Erdélyi. They were people of great erudition and eloquence, we were very fond of them. Both were executed by the partisans.

József Bogner was for a while headmaster of the students' dorm. He became a teacher after the town was reattached to Hungary and later became the Mayor of the town. His elder sister was a nun called Margit Bogner. Her suit for beatification is in progress now.

After the fighting, there were three students from the grammar school who were leaders of the occupying partisan groups: Radak Milos, Jelics Dusan and Dezső Pintér (his father was Hungarian, his mother Serbian but he declared himself a Serb). As far as we know, the week before the executions they had József Bognár repair all the clocks of the partisans, since he also had a

127

watchmaker's certificate. At early dawn, he was executed together
with László Erdélyi. It is said that their judge and the executor of
the verdict was Dezső Pintér."

   "Several days after they arrived, news began to spread that so
and so was taken away and killed. On a November night we were
wakened by a loud pounding. Peeping through the slits in the
shutters, we heard that our neighbors were directing the armed
men to the house at the corner. That was when I saw men and
women pressed together on a peasant horse cart. The cart stopped
in front of our house. Holding our breath, we were wondering
what was to happen since my father was leader of the Turán
Hunters in Szabadka. He had been imprisoned once for two years
for the Hungarian cause in Serbian times, for which he also got
the Hungarian National Defence Cross after 1941. People were
killed for lesser "crimes" than that . It was on this night that
Dévavári was taken from next door, then the shoemaker Elizák
from the other end of the street. It was also this night that the Kiss
brothers and János Csiszár disappeared; they never came back. It
was one of those days that the wholesale merchant Géza Nojcsek,
president of the Hungarian Readers Circle, was killed.
   They also killed our teacher of Hungarian, László Erdélyi, who
had just come home as a Reserve Lance Sergeant. He was
wounded in the arm during a shooting at the station. His old
Serbian students took him to the first aid station, then took him
home; they assured him he was safe. Unfortunately, as word
spread around town, one student, who the teacher had failed,
hired a thirteen-year old lad to take him away. He was never seen
alive again.
   What could István Kuden have done? He was a Czech, who did
not speak perfect Hungarian and served art as a double-bass
player in the theater orchestra of the Hungarian Readers Circle. It
might have been since living on Párhuzamos Street, in the ghetto
area and being a hobby gardener, he refused someone a lettuce.
   During the first elections at the courthouse, one could look at the
list of people who were eliminated. I did not dare to look at the
list, but my mother went ti see if my father and my brother would
be on it. Some one thousand names were listed, but the list was
rather inaccurate and our people were not on it. The list was hung
in three rooms each labelled "enemies of the people", "traitors" or
"Fascists". Where this list is or whether it still exists at all, no one
knows."

   In 1948, one could inquire about those who had disappeared. It was István Vukovics, later president of the Supreme Court of Vojvodina who, in 1944, announced that all those who had "disappeared" were dead. The authorities were willing to certify the innocence of those who had been certifiably executed wrongly. During the first days of the distribution of the certificates there was such an onslaught of relatives at the court that the president, fearing rebellion, stopped the distribution of rehabilitation papers. Those who did not get one then, would regret it later. Many, out of hatred for the murderers, did not ask for papers testifying to the innocence of their relatives. Many of them paid for it, since they could not prove the innocence of those who had been executed, they were deprived of all their belongings.

Among the executed people, there were many in transit; these people were seized at the station. Those who could not certify themselves were promptly executed. It was chiefly the Hungarian soldiers or deserters from the army that fell victim to their desire for freedom.

APATIN - KULA

In Apatin would have been no reason for reprisals since no one was killed when the Hungarians came in, yet some three hundred people were killed by the partisans. Some of them on the spot, but the majority were taken to Zombor to the notorious Kronich Palace, where a favorite means of torture was making captives run on hot coals; the name of the chief torturer was not forgotten, Zika Laszics. Those who were burnt in this way knew that the next day they would be shot either by the Danube or on the race course. Those who were not taken to Zombor were taken to prison camps by the hundreds. There they died of hunger or of different diseases. Some survived, only todie from the greasy feast in their honor; when they returned to their home, their stomach just could not take it. That is how the number rose to three hundred.

In 1941, a big celebration was held on the main square of Kula. The parish priest came with his curate. When the chief spokesman began to abuse the Serbians, the priest left the square in protest and hardly veiled disapproval; his curate joined him. The incident was not forgotten by the Serbians present who on December 11 and 13, during the days of the Kula massacres; they took the priest under their protection. They executed more than five hundred Hungarians at the time, chiefly intellectuals but also

the wealthy craftsmen, merchants and farmers (class enemies?!).
Some farms were robbed and ruined. Some mass graves keep
the secrets of those bloody days.

WHERE THERE WAS A RECONCILIATION

In Bajsa the honest, benevolent Serbians and the more common
types were at variance with one another. The mob was getting
ready for a large scale massacre of the Hungarians. In the first
place, they wanted to execute Béla Németh the parish priest, with
long preparations. They had already had him dig his grave at the
end of the village. The grave was not a very honorable one, and
the armed men were still argued whether it would be deep or wide
enough. When the more sober Serbians arrived, they wrenched
the rifles out of the hands of the vulgar rabble. Once the priest
was released, they reminded the others of 1941, when the
Hungarians stood up for their Serbian fellows.

Kispiac could see a spectacular change in the behavior of a man
full of hatred. The Serbians of Kispiac District also gathered to
agree on the extermination of Hungarians. The spokesman for the
extremists was a widely known enemy of the Hungarians,
Milosev Zivo. Everyone knew that he had already caused them
much bitterness in Royal Yugoslavia. For such sedition, he had
been arrested and detained in Martonos in 1941. Pál Galgóczi, a
Hungarian who he had hurt, attacked him with a knife and
wounded him in the neck, but they were separated in time to save
Zivo's life. Galgóczi apologized, and Milosev was very much
moved by this; he who had recourse to physical violence on the
man in the arrogance of his power. Galgóczi asked the Hungarian
Court to release his old enemy. This mutual reconciliation
persisted between them from 41 to 44, when the Serbians of
Kispiac flocked to massacre the Hungarians. Under the influence
of their changed leader, they ended by executing no one. They did
not even torture a single person among the rounded-up
Hungarians.

Nemes Miletics (Svetozar Miletics), was famous for the fact
that there was peace between the Serbians and the Hungarians. In
1941, it was the Hungarians who dissuaded the gendarmes from
implementing their more severe plans, and in 1944 it was the
Serbians who persuaded their partisans that there was no need in
Miletics to massacre Hungarians.

THE SZEKELYS RUN THE GAUNTLET

The situation of the Bukovina Székelys had become critical in October 1944, while scattered to twenty-five villages of Bácska. The authorities did not warn the people of the impending danger. Although there were fires burning from time to time on farms, as well as the criminal attempts of the Dobrovoljacs in 1941, warned the Székelys that their quiet farming life would not last very long.

Ádám Sebestyén writes the following in his memoir entitled **"Flight of the People of Andrásfalva from Bácska."**

"Towards the end of September, the situation had become chaotic; the partisans started to endanger the life of the peaceful peasants. Fear spread because of the night raids on the village volks; the leaders disguised the real situation.

The Andrásmező people were preparing for a fair on October 8th. They kept cooking and baking, expecting guests. Those headed for the houses of their friends received the horrible news; they had to run!

Orders to evacuate their homes came late; there was hardly any time to pack. There was an enormous pell-mell confusion; they had but two or three hours to think. People did not know what to pack for the family in their haste; they had to decide between food, clothes, or furniture. Many of them were not able to leave until the next morning. They had to leave things behind, just when they had become a bit better off; when the barns were full of corn, the lofts full of wheat and other grains. The sties were full of pigs weighing between one hundred and fifty and two hundred kilos. Some farmers left behind as many as fifteen or twenty pigs; a small fortune for them.

They had no idea where they were going to sleep the following day. On the roads, with the German army retreating, cart after cart fled from the Soviet army, together with cars and tanks obstructing one another. They had frequent air raids and the army was trying to force the poor families off the road. A lot of women bore their children on the road, many labored on corn hills. They were even robbed by malevolent people. On a pitch dark night, even the coffin of one grandfather was stolen. Only at dawn did the son find the coffin cast on the edge of a ditch with the body of the father.

The escapees of Andrásfalva, who could not cross the Danube on the ferry because of the tumult, were sent by the army to Paks and Dunaföldvár. During the air raids that came, when they were crossing a lot of children lost their parents and could only find them weeks later. They fled towards Dombovár, but they did not accept Szálasi's advice to go to Germany."

Many people hastily killed and cut up a pig to provide the family with food on the road. They could not prepare the meat anywhere so it rotted in the cart and they threw the pork into the Danube.

When the partisans met the packed carts they made good use of these opportunities by robbing the wretched people of their meager belongings. After robbing the people, they drove them to camps or let them go with the shirts on their backs." The losses of the Székelys of the twenty-five villages have not been counted to this day. We could only count and list the victims of the people of Hadikliget. Sándor Sára made a film of their struggle to get north, entitled "At the Crossroads." interviewing widows, and other survivors. Gábor Albert also wrote about them in his book "Head Up."

A man from Hadikliget, Titusz Várda, had rare luck in surviving his fellows:

"We set off from Hadikliget on October 8, 1944, Our deceitful, half-Serbian leader took us to Szabadka instead of Zombor. At the cemetery of Szabadka we were stopped by the partisans. They told us to take the cows, cart, horses to the Palics barracks. We had to leave all our valuable possessions and were taken into custody. A few days later, they rounded up some five hundred of us in a pub. The pubkeeper was beaten up, thrown out and the partisans drank everything while they kept themselves busy with the Székelys. From there, they took the women and children to the mill, where they had to sit on the cold concrete, and the males were taken to the prison of Szabadka.

They kept on asking me what I was doing for a living. I said I was a hired man. I was showing them my hands, but they were by no means nice to me. I really did not have land at the time, thank God. I was given the classification number 2, while forty -three received the number 1. What it actually meant we did not know until the others were hoarded on a truck. All of them were executed, as far as we know, and were buried in the knacker's yard of Szabadka. The previous day we had seen a large pit there. In thirty minutes the truck came back empty. It was the partisans who had taken them, there were no Russians. They had put a machine gun on this truck. They lined us up and were shooting away above our heads. There were some who wet their pants in fear.

While the women were cooking, the children stood by very hungry. A partisan came up and defecated into the pot. A big-bellied man, Fazekas, was made to stand up, and was tossed about until he collapsed. They accused him of having grown fat on the Serbians' blood.

Once I was questioned by a partisan woman. She was laying on her back asking questions. She asked me if I was related to Tito since my name is Titusz. I did not protest as she laughed. They gave me a paper saying I was free to go where I wanted to in Szabadka, since I had the number two and my name is Titusz. Not much later, we were put on a train to Baja. The list of Székelys from Hadikliget who were murdered at Szabadka is as follows:

1.Fábián Antal	
2.Lajos Antal	23.Lajos Jakab
3.Ferenc Barabás	24.István Kiss
4.Gáspár Bece	25.Piusz Kökény
5.István Biró	26.István Lovas
6.Ambrus Cseke	27.Rudolf Lovas
7.Márton Csiki	28.Orbán Lovász
8.Antal Eris	29.Pál Mátyás
9.Géza Erős	30.Piusz Mátyás
10.János Erős	31.János Miklós
11.Boldizsár Fazekas	32.Vilmos Miklós
12.Lajos Fazekas	33.Antal Nagy
13.Piusz Fazekas	34.Lőrinc Nagy
14.József Ferenc	35.Vilmos Sólymosi
15.Márton Forrai	36.István Szabó
16.Márton Forrai Sn.	37.József Szabó
17.Sándor Forrai	38.Ágoston Szentes
18.Antal Illés	39.Jeromos Szentes
19.Gergely Illés	40.Antal Venczel
20.István Illés	41.Gergely Venczel
21.József Illés	42.Géza Zalavári
22.Fábián Jakab	43.Péter Zalavári

THE PETŐFI BRIGADE

It is impossible to diminish the glory of military troops who won battles, even after several decades as long as the "heroes" or their followers safeguarding their memory are alive. The official communist party hack historians regarded the Petőfi Brigade as a heroic contribution to the Yugoslavian liberation movement of the Tito Regime. The Hungarians of Bácska had ambivalent feelings about the creation of the brigade, in a situation of constant danger of the massacres.

Let us look back to those long years when the enthusiasm of Hungarians for the Yugoslavian cause had to be identified with the "voluntary"contribution of the Hungarian people to the Titoist State System:

The creation of the Sándor Petőfi Battalion was instituted by the High Command of the Croatian Liberation Army and that of the Second Detachment of Partisan troops in Slavonia in August 1943. Some eighty Hungarians joined up in the beginning. In this and the following year the ever growing battalion fought together with the other communist detachments along the Drava River. Its chief task was the mobilization of the Hungarians of the provinces under Tito's control.

Those who, in wartime, could or would keep contact with the minuscule left-wing population of Budapest and its radical sentiments, will know and remember how fashionable it was to sympathize with the "Yugo" partisans. Among the young waiting to be enlisted or to be called up to one of the labor battalions; it was believed that it was lot smarter to cross the Drava and join the partisans, than to fight the Soviet army on the Eastern front. There were a few people who got into the rowboats and crossed over to the right bank of the river. There were also some brave people who supplied or tried to supply bandages, medicine and ammunition to the partisans over the Drava.

In November 1944 the battalion named after Sándor Petőfi, the well known Hungarian poet of the 1848-49 Revolution marched into the Pécs-Siklós-Moslavina area, and was incorporated into the 16th Detachment of Vojvodina.

"In October, at the liberation of Bácska, the Vojvodinan leaders of the Communist Party announced: *Everything for the front, everyone to the front!* The Party used the same slogan to recruit people of Hungarian nationality into the Yugoslavian Liberating Army. For this purpose the party organization of Bácstopolya sent two deputies to Novi Sad to see General Kosta Nadj, Commander in Chief of the Yugoslavian Liberating Army and of the staff of the Vojvodinan partisan troops. The deputies asked General Nadj to give permission to create the Hungarian Brigade in Vojvodina. They suggested that, after the example of the Slavonian Hungarian Battalion, they name it after Sándor Petőfi.

The creation of the Hungarian Brigade was instituted by an order of the High Command on November 23, 1944."

It is not known whether the two party members from Topolya gave an account of the fact, that the partisans in their territory had already tortured and executed 360 Hungarians. They did say that in 1941 some seventy Serbians from Topolya lost their lives in the shootings.

Even if they admitted that it was a vendetta five times over; as a threat, they suggested to the Hungarians that they become partisans, just to give them their chance to remain alive.

In the light of these facts, can we judge the following"

"The voluntary recruiting activities of the party activists in Bácstopolya spread fast in all of Bácska. Hundreds of people volunteered from Topolya, Moravica, Csantavér, Ada, Mohol, Feketics, Zenta, Kishegyes, Bajsa, Pacsér, Bajmok and some other places too. Nothing proves the "enthusiasm" better than the fact that in a few days nine hundred people volunteered.

In some cases the father volunteered with his son or daughter. From certain families two or three brothers took up arms. As an example as many as six male members from the Óvári family put their names on the list of volunteers."

We can have no reason to doubt their enthusiasm, but we are pretty well aware of the horrible circumstances. **These unfortunate men understood well that they could choose of between the brigade and death.**

In Topolya a small monument marks the spot, the brigade started for Zombor, but the mass grave in the swamp of the old pond, above which a tennis court has been built, remains unmarked.

The Hungarian "volunteers" of Bácska and the Slavonian Hungarian partisans met on December 20 in Felsőszentmárton. They first lined up for parade on December 31, 1944 as soldiers of the newly formed 15th.

Vojvodinan brigade named after Sándor Petőfi. There were 1,200 of them some not yet equipped with guns. There were some who got disillusioned on the way and deserted. Perhaps they were afraid not only for their own lives but for their families' lives too. These people did not throw a favorable light on the brigade. When they got home they complained about the way they had been treated and about the future of the brigade.

In reaction to the alarming news spread by the escapees, the "Free Vojdovina" of Novi Sad printed the following on January 18th, 1944:

"Several hundred Hungarian males and females from Topolya entered the Petìfi Brigade voluntarily to take up arms against Fascism. These Hungarian troops are fighting somewhere in Transdanubia. Some irresponsible people are spreading news that the brigade was for the most part dissolved. The United People's Front of Topolya sent out Dezső Sinkovics to meet those members of the brigade who were from Topolya and to bring letters from them to reassure their families. Sinkovics brought a letter with the signatures of all. Now from the letter:

"We want to destroy Fascism and build a new democratic state and we want to be worthy of the name of our brigade and of Marshal Tito, the most perfect partisan of peace... Let the cowards spreading false information shake in terror. Those who, by their escape and by besmirching the fair name of our brigade, support the Fascists. We will be there at the show-down, and woe to the traitors. We will wash this filth off the honour of the Hungarian nation with the blood of our traitors!"

However, the show-down with the traitors came about in a different way than promised in the letter, which must have been written by the commissar. The escapees were rounded up in several weeks' time. Led by István Varga they were taken back to the corps, which was fighting in the neighborhood of Bolmány and had already suffered losses. It was in Baranya, Bolmány, that the brigade, now three times as numerous, clashed with the detachment of the well equipped retreating German Balkan Army, marching towards Transdanubia and Budapest.

The survivors created legends about their battles; evaluation is not our task:

According to General Kosta Nadj there were fifty killed and one hundred and ninety wounded. The number is small if we consider later rumors, that the Serbian generals had the brigade massacred by the German SS corps.

According to other sources, in the March battles, lasting for one week, nine tenths of the brigade was annihilated. Those who survived were enlisted in other partisan units. Whether it happened this way or another, it is true that the remaining soldiers were sent to other corps.

At the end of 1944, and the beginning of 1945, the German Balkan Army tried to cross the Danube first, to approach the Hungarian capital through Bácska. When they failed, they assailed the Drava west of Eszék (Osiek), and they did cross temporarily to the left bank.

But remembering the alarming news spread in Topolya, we should not forget their attempts to cross the Danube in the beginning of 1945. Our correspondent enlisted with exceptional luck, as a clerk to a Serbian military workers' detachment in Szabadka.

Our platoon was stationed stationed on the Danube cutting an acacia forest, because, they heated the wagons with wood. We were lodged in peasant houses.

One night we saw soldiers marching by, four abreast, in tattered clothes from the station. The feet of some were covered in rags speaking Hungarian. When we asked them who they were, they said they belonged to the Petőfi Brigade from Topolya. When we asked them where they were going. they said they were going to the front. "Without a gun?" I asked one of them in wonderment. He said, ecchoing the commissar: "The Germans have guns, we have to take them from them!"

The front line in those days was between Ilok and Sarengrad. The Germans had a powerful artillery against the Serbian trenches. In front of us, the terrain was full of landmines. The Petőfi Brigade was needed to neutralize the mines. The people were driven onto the mine field at night. One could hear the sporadic explosions. At eight in the morning, a messenger came to me bringing an order that the workers' detachments should go to the Danube to pick up the casualties. No statistics were made of the people who lost their lives there..."

REPORT OF LOSSES

In addition to our extensive gathering of data, the investigations of two brave Roman Catholic Priests have offered the most reliable source of information. Márton Szücs, retired Dean of Bácsszőllős, and József Kovács, retired Parson of Martonos, had dedicated the last years of their life for gathering the data of the innocent Hungarians executed in Bácska in the autumn of 1944. They used the official registry books of the parishes of Bácska and the recollections of eyewitness parishioners.

The title of their work is **"The Silence of the Dead"**, a requiem in memory of the innocent victims. Their own physical fear of reprisal was also included in the title. The publishing of their summary was authorized after their death.

The gathering of data took place in the greatest of possible secrecy, because of the Yugoslavian security forces and the prohibition of publishing the details of the war crimes by the authorities.

Further difficulties were caused by the fact, that in most of the villages of Bácska, the terrorized Hungarians kept an incomplete register (Csurog, Novi Sad, Zsablya, Szabadka). Although the data provided was very close to the exact figures, the data of these places are accompanied by the caveat: **Appr.** (approximately) on the lists.

In another column are listed those communities, where the inhabitants could recall the number of victims with an accuracy of plus or minus 10. These are labeled with the sign: **a.e.** (almost exact). In the smaller villages, where the dead were remembered by name and number, they receive the sign: **e.** (exact).

Our headings originate from the two devout Catholic priests in their edition in the order of the Serbian village names. The register discloses the data of Serbs, Communists and Jews slain and executed between 1941 and 1944. The data had been compiled by Yugoslavian organizations; we can not vouch for their accuracy.

The data published here of the number of Hungarians executed by the partisan gangs in 1944, are the results of the research of the two Priests.

The register reveals the data of the research in eight columns. Apart from the names of the communities, a certain subjectivity cannot be excluded among the data of Columns 2 and 6.

138

The Columns of the Chart:
1. The name of the locality
2. The number of slain Serbian chetniks and armed resisters during the reentry of Hungarian military forces in 1941
3. The number of dead during the incarceration 1941 and 1944.
4. Died at the hands of the counter intelligence of Novi Sad.
5. Executed during the raids.
6. The total sum of casualties from 1941 to 1944.
7. The number of Hungarians massacred in the 1944.
8. Qualification of the exactitude of the gathered data.

The seventh column abounds in question marks. These question marks in many cases hide the sorrow of undiscovered and unconfessed crimes. As a result of our research, we have managed to erase some of these question marks.

The list of communities includes some villages inhabited by Hungarians outside Bácska as well.

Serbian name	Hungarian Name	No2	No3	No4	No5	No6	No7	No8
Ada	Ada	17	0	2	0	19	16	e
Adorjan	Adorjan	0	0	0	0	0	58	e
Alel. Sentic		0	46	3	0	49	0	e
Apatin	Apatin	0	0	0	0	0	300	ne
Bacs	Bacs	0	3				3	
Palanka	Bacspalanka	0	0	5		5	300	app
Topolya	Bacstopolya	70	0	0	0	70	360	ae
B. Breg	Bereg	0	3	0	0	3	?	
B. Berestovac	Szilberek	0	0	1	0	1	0	
B.Gracac	Szentfulop	0	0	0	0	0	240	e
B. Monostor	Monostorszeg	0	1	1	0	2	?	
B. Petrovac	Petroc	1	0	9	0	10	?	
B. Vinogradi	Bacsszolos	0	0	0	0	0	12	e
B. Gradiste	Bacsfoldvar	7	0	7	0	14	70	e
B. Petr. Selo	Peterreve	4	0	6	0	10	600	ae
Bajmok	Bajmok	8	25	0	0	33	80	e
Bajsa	Bajsa	0	0	0	0	0	0	
Becej	Obecse	7	0	40	206	253	500	app
Beli Monastir	Pelmonostor	0	0	2	0	2	?	
Bezdan	Bezdan	0	0	0	0	0	183	e
Bodjani	Bogyan	0	0	0	0	0	8	ae
Bogojevo	Gombos	0	0	0	0	0	20	e
Bolman	Bolmany	0	0	2	0	2	?	
Budislava	Tiszakalmanfalva	0	0	0	0	0	10	e

139

Serbian name	Hungarian Name	No2	No3	No4	No5	No6	No7	No8
Buklin	Dunabokeny	1	0	0	0	0	?	
Crvenka	Cservenka	13	0	0	0	13	?	
Cantavir	Csantaver	0	0	0	0	0	10	e
Conoplja	Csonoplya	0	0	0	0	00	17	e
Curog	Csurog	15	0	26	765	806	3000	app
Darda	Darda	0	0	1	0	1	?	
Deronje	Dernye	0	0	2	0	2	?	
D.Sv.Ivan	Urszentivan	2	0	3	0	5	?	
Doroslovo	Doroszlo	0	0	0	0	0	10	e
Dubosevica	Dalyok	0	0	3	0	3	?	
Djurdjevo	Sajkasgyorgye	1	0	32	212	244	?	
Feketic	Bacsfeketehegy	4	10	0	0	14	?	
Futog	Futak	0	0	6	0	6	?	
Glozan	Dunagalos	0	0	3	0	3	?	
Gospodinci	Boldogasszonyfalva	0	0	23	0	78	?	
Gardinovci	Dunagardony	1	0	1	38	40	?	
Horgos	Horgos	22	0	0	0	22	60	e
Kac	Katy	0	0	1	0	1	?	
Kanjiza	Magyarkanizsa	13	0	0	0	13	75	e
Kelebia	Kelebia	4	0	0	0	4	?	
Kisac	Kiszacs	0	0	6	0	6	?	
Kovilj	Alsokabol	1	0	15	0	16	8	
Kruscic	Veprod	0	0	0	0	0	9	e
Kula	Kula	49	0	3	0	52	500	ae
Kulpin	Kolpeny	0	0	1	0	1	?	
Kupusina	Bacskertes	0	0	0	0	0	10	e
Lalic	Liliomos	0	0	1	0	1	?	
Lok	Sajkaslak	0	0	0	46	46	28	e
Mali Idos	Kishegyes	1				1		e
Martonos	Martonos	0	0	0	0	0	24	e
Mol	Mohol	13	0	0	0	13	600	ae
Mosorin	Mozsor	2	1	1	175	183	72	e
Nadalj	Nadalja	0	0	2	0	2	?	
Novi Sad	Ujvidek	159	0	67	808	1094	10000	app
Pacir	Pacser	16	0	0	0	16	200	ae
Palic	Palicsfurdo	20	0	0	0	20	?	
Parage	Parrag	0	0	2	0	2	?	
Pivnice	pinced	0	0	1	0	1	?	
Plavna	Palona	7	0	0	0	7	8	
Popovac	Baranyavar	0	50	4	0	54	?	
Rastina	Kortes	2	0	0	0	2	?	
Sokolac	Nerasolymos	2	2	0	0	4	?	
Senta	Zenta	52	21	5	0	78	87	e

Serbian name	Hungarian Name	No2	No3	No4	No5	No6	No7	No8
Silbas	Szilbacs	1	0	3	0	4	?	
Sirig	Szoreg	100	0	0	0	100	?	
Sivac	Szivacs	0	0	5	0	5	74	e
Sombor	Zombor	0	0	11	0	11	5650	app
Sonta	szond	0	0	0	0	0	3	e
Srbobran	Szenttamas	92	12	21	3	128	2000	app
Stapar	Sztapar	0	0	4	0	4	?	
St. Moravica	Bacskossuthfalva	1	0	0	0	2	0	e
Stepanicevo		1	0	0	0	1		
Subotica	Szabadka	147	15	18	0	180	7000	app
Svilojevo	Szilagyi	0	0	0	0	0	?	
Sajkas	Sajkas	8	0	4	0	12	?	
Sove	Osove	0	0	4	0	4	?	
Tavankut	Tavankut	0	0	0	0	16		
Temerin	Temerin	3	30	0	39	72	480	app
Titel	Titel	2	0	6	52	60	54	e
Totovo	Totfalu	1	0	1	0	2	?	
Tovarisevo	Bacstovaros	1	0	1	0	2	?	
Tresnjevac		0	0	0	0	0	13	e
Turja	Turja	0	0	5	0	5	?	
Vajska	Vajszka	0	0	0	0	0	13	e
Vrbas	Ujverbasz	5	0	3	0	8	10	e
Vilovo	Tunderes	0	0	1	63	64	?	
Zmajevo	Oker	1	0	1	0	2	-	e
Zmajevac	Vorosmart	0	0	1	0	1	?	
Zabalj	Zsablya	0	0	29	381	610	2000	app
Odzaci	Hodsag	0	0	0	0	0	183	e
	TOTAL	876	219	404	3130	4629	34491	

The list of the villages comes from The Silence of the Dead

Summarized register of Serbs and Jews disappeared
between 1941 and 1944:

Killed in action in 1941	876 persons
Died during deportations	219 "
Died in Counter-intell. custody	404 "
Executed in the raid of 1942	3,130 "
Total number of Serbian and Jewish dead	4,629 persons

Taken to reception camps	7,865 persons
Taken to labor camps	2,116 "
Mobilized	1,677 "
Total affected	11,658 persons

141

Source: Zlocini okupatora u Vojvodini, Volume I., Novi Sad, 1946.

We are obliged to disclose the total number of Yugoslavian casualties published in 1946. However, its figures do not correspond with the available Hungarian official data in every respect.
On the other hand:

The Hungarian casualties in the autumn of 1944, reach a total sum of 34,491.
If we add the thousands executed in the uninvestigated, unexamined 40 villages to our deathlist, the number will certainly exceed forty thousand.

Roman Catholic priests and friars executed in the end of 1944:
1. Antal Berger, Tavankút
2. Bálint Dupp, Curog
3. Pál Göncöl, Sirig
4. István Köves, Mosorin
5. József Novotny, Plevna
6. Ferenc Petrényi, Becse
7. Ferenc Plank, Sivac
8. Dénes Szabó, Totovo Selo
9. Ferenc Takács, B. Petr. Selo.
10. Lajos Varga, Mohol
11. István Virág, Horgos
12. Mihály Werner, Martonos

Franciscan friars
1. Krizosztom Körösztös
2. Kristóf Kovács, monastery of Novi Sad and
3. Ferenc Fleisz, monastery of Szabadka

142

VERDICTS AFTER REVENGE

The relatives of the executed kept terrified silence about the bloody reprisals in Bácska in the Autumn of 1944. Those who escaped to Hungary dared only to whisper in fear the horrors they had experienced in their own immediate environs.

The approximate summary of the massacres originates from brave priests, who turned with their experiences to the authority accessible to them, the Cardinal of Esztergom, the Prince Primate József Mindszenty; they expected some help. The Cardinal addressed a letter to the Hungarian Foreign Minister, who was making preparations for the peace negotiations, and wrote about the massacre of 40,000-50,000 innocent Hungarians in Bácska.

Foreign Minister János Gyöngyösi, as far as I know, never took advantage of this report in any of his speeches, memorandas, negotiations, though it is certain that he shared the contents of the Cardinal's letter with at least his party and the significant persons of his coalition government.

It is probable, that nobody dared to accuse the highly respected Josip Broz Tito. In the West and in the East the guerilla leader was esteemed so highly, that it was impossible even to mention any of the genocides committed by his troops and gangs of partisans on Croatians, Slovenians, Germans or Hungarians.

The grievances suffered by Hungarians in Bácska in 1944 did not even turn up during the trials dealing with the atrocities of the Hungarian Counter Intelligence police at Novi Sad nor in the peace negotiations.

It is characteristic of the humiliating fear of the democratic Hungarian government, that Prime Minister Ferenc Nagy in the beginning of 1947, was required to deliver about 3,500 inhabitants of Bácska to the Yugoslavian authorities; they were regarded as fugitives. In addition, he gave opportunity and permission for a far reaching OZNA investigation on Hungarian territory. The majority of the fugitives handed over to the Serbians were executed.

Was Ferenc Szombathelyi, former chief of the general staff, aware of the annihilation of many thousands of Hungarians in Bácska? He wanted to deny his responsibility for the the massacre at Novi Sad in the 1945 autobiographical memoranda before being arrested, by the American authorities for war crimes.

"In the bloody events at Novi Sad and Bácska, writes

Szombathelyi, a great many Hungarians, especially the right wingers and most of the staff officers, saw a great national exploit. They thought of the events as strong arm measures, normal under special guerilla wartime conditions. Unfortunately, I could not alter the situation, because the events had been so horrible that I could not turn to the public with them nor could I release any propaganda statements. The public opinion of the country was entirely under the influence of right wing propaganda, and developed in accordance with it. I would not have thought that the events at Novi Sad had been so terrible, and for a long time I did not believe so, though I never made the mistake of regarding the events at Novi Sad as exploits. I had been convinced for a long time, that there had been a justified reprisal by the troops, which would put an end to Serbian atrocities committed against the Hungarian public security; the administrative organisations; and property damages.

There would be peace at last on this land, which was disturbed by the Serbs and not us, because they did not intend to sympathize with our peaceful and tolerant administration based on the ideas of St. Stephen. What is more they opposed it completely.

In contrast with all the others, I believed the reports of the responsible commanders, namely Generals Feketehalmy-Czeydner and Grassy, who had led the events on the spot, and whom I had known as honest, reliable soldiers up till now. They constantly denied in writing, as well as in words, that there had been bloodshed. If occasionally debauchery had taken place, the reason for that had plainly been the provocative behaviour of the Serb population. I could never get a report from them of the number and identity of the casualties, but they denied that many had been killed, and that women and children had been among them.

I thought I had been delivered an exaggerated report by the civil service. Civil servants get frightened easily, and cry for the armed forces. When the armed forces take severe measures, which cause casualties, they grow even more frightened and would prefer to decline responsibility. They regard the events as ones which did not happen at all.

Considering the international situation mainly in relation to Germany; the Serbian internecine massacres of the partisan movements within our borders; what the Serbs had to suffer at the hands of the German and Croatian troops; and consequently developing homicidal psychosis, I did not find it wise nor did I find the time convenient to call attention to such a scandalous case, which would have completely ruined the peace of the whole country. The government refused to stir up the matter. I was too young a chief to risk such a great battle on my own, which much later, after having discovered the truth entirely, I lost. I laid the matter aside in accordance with government wishes; I pleaded for its shelving by the Regent.

I did not initiate the mopping up operation at Novi Sad; it was the Ministry of the Interior with whom I maintained close contact throughout the whole operation in Bácska. I informed them of everything I learned from the military line. When he reported to me, I ordered Feketehalmy-Czeydner to personally report to the Minister for Home Affairs and to the Prime Minister. He had been briefed by both Ministers before the operation at Novi Sad

After the events at Novi Sad, my conviction grew firm, that attrocities had taken place on the part of the military forces. Eventually I had to acknowledge the fact, that I had been misled by the reports, and my subordinates could be accused with dereliction of duty and negligence.

On the basis of police reports; private information; and the conclusions reached by my attorneys; it was beyond doubt, that an awful crime had been committed.

The crime had not only taken the lives of wretched Serbian casualties, but we Hungarians also had to suffer a terrible blow. As a commanding officer, I could only declare it a real "national catastrophe". This realization caused me a terrible disappointment in my respected comrades and staff officers. When I reached the end of the road of sorrowful realization, I acted firmly and mercilessly. I transformed the whole matter into a personal one; I put the matter before the court of the chief of staff. Although my Prosecutor was against it, I made a charge of disloyalty.

I did not want too much publicity nor did I want to burden anybody with this difficult case, which lived on in the public opinion as a falsely interpreted national act of heroism. I did not find anybody else with the necessary strength fit to settle the matter. I could not decline responsibility, because it was a matter which concerned the whole country.

The Minister for Home Affairs warned me, that this was not the concern of the court of the chief of staff, because it was not the case of disloyalty but ordinary murder and robbery. I was afraid that in someone else's hands the judgement would be delayed or even dropped.

Since I was the highest commander of the Hungarian Army, it was my duty to settle it. I had to shoulder the damage suffered by the honour of the Hungarian arms and the Hungarian soldier. I have to point out, that I was severely attacked by the Kállay government. The fact that I took the matter seriously is well shown in the selection of the members of the court; the severity of the verdicts; the extension of the charge; the news bulletins; my orders to my officers; my informative and enlightening speeches; and those articles that appeared after the German occupation of Hungary in right wing papers; the intense interest of the German military attache during the trial; and finally my own arrest and arraignment.

I did not arrest generals Feketehalmy-Czeydner and Grassy, and this enabled them to escape to Germany. The reason for this is as follows: first of all, I seldom consented to my prosecutors' suggestion of arrest, except for cases concerning financial affairs, because I have always esteemed human freedom and dignity highly. Since my own arrest, I see how right I had been. I have respected Generals Feketehalmy-Czeydner and Grassy. They were Hungarian generals, comrades, who I did not want to put under arrest. Both were glad to have their case put before the court as soon as possible. I regarded the arrest just as unworthy of a Hungarian general, as his later escape, but there was one problem I had to take into consideration.

Behind the whole affair stood the Germans as the likely original instigators, who wanted to prevent us at any price from having good relations with our neighbors. They took advantage of this affair at Novi Sad by creating an eternal anymosity between the Hungarians and the Serbs. They would have rescued the two Hungarian protagonists even by force. Unfortunately I have to say that they could have succeeded, because public opinion regarded the two as national heroes.

I did not want to provoke such a forced liberation; I did not want to initiate a fight that I could only lose. I had to consider also the Minister of National Defence, Mr. Bartha. He did not want the trial of Novi Sad, either, probably due to his right wing sentiments. It was also a gesture towards him not to have ordered the arrests, but to have displayed reasonableness in the carrying out of the verdicts.

With their escape and with the abandoning of their subordinates, Generals Feketehalmy-Czeydner and Grassy imposed judgement upon themselves. I wanted to try everything possible, so that they could defend themselves freely without any obstacles. For once not only their own honour, but the honour of the whole Hungarian nation and the Hungarian arms was at stake. I gave special orders to the court to ensure fairness. In the interest of defense of the gendarme officers, I ordered the gendarme general to take part on the trial, but I forbade the participation of right wing politicians.

That the affair at Novi Sad was also a German one is well
proven by the fact that the two protagonists were saved by the
Germans. Although they had been demoted in the Hungarian
Army, they were promoted in the German General Staff, thus
giving rise to the prestige of the "Hungarian heroes". After the
occupation of Hungary, the Germans extracted the release and
acquittal of the condemned; and the rehabilitation of Generals
Feketehalmy and Grassy. They became Hungarian generals again,
and I was arrested, imprisoned and charged."

The American military forces delivered Szombathelyi to the
Hungarian government as a war criminal, so that he could answer
for his actions during the war before the People's Court of
Budapest. The People's Court, after a four day open trial,
sentenced Ferenc Szombathelyi to ten years imprisonment. It is
worth quoting some details from the reasons adduced:

"In the reannexed Southern Territories, as has been stated in the
verdict against Prime Minister Bárdossy, the Serbian rebels
threatened public security; treacherously murdered Hungarian
soldiers and security officials. The situation deteriorated to such a
point, that the local security organizations proved insufficient for
the restoration of order. For this reason the Minister for Home
Affairs pleaded for military reinforcements. Bárdossy, put in
charge the Minister of National Defence, directing the military
forces to clear the South of the rebels in cooperation with the
civilian administration.

General Szombathelyi ordered the commanding general of the
South, (the commander of the army corps of Szeged), General
Feketehalmy-Czeydner, to head the operation aimed at the
restoration of order in Bácska. For his assistance, he asked them
to form a commission, which the Minister for Home Affairs
rejected, claiming that there are the Lord Lieutenants for this
purpose. He succeeded in having Representative Popovics
appointed next to Feketehalmy-Czeydner as an adviser with the
consent of the Minister for Home Affairs. This time it was
Feketehalmy-Czeydner who rejected it, because he regarded the
person in question as pro German. In spite of his instructions, he
completely ignored the Lord Lieutenants. The accused had no
special intentions concerning the South; from the military point of
view, mopping up was not necessary.

In connection with the events in Zabalj, he received reports of a
serious battle from Feketehalmy-Czeydner. He began to think that
after all there was a military operation going on. After finishing
the mopping up operation in Zabalj, the Minister for Home Affairs
thought it necessary to extend the mopping up to Novi Sad as

well. For this purpose he asked for army units again from the Minister of National Defense. Granting the request, the accused once again appointed Feketehalmy-Czeydner as Commander. According to his defence, if he had known what had happened in Zabalj, he would not have given armed forces for the mopping up operation at Novi Sad.

He was misled by false reports from Feketehalmy-Czeydner. Before his activity in Novi Sad, Feketehalmy-Czeydner had received the instructions in Budapest from the Minister for Home Affairs, the Minister of National Defense, and from the accused, but had not received any special instructions. His reports, did not mention the cruelties of the armed forces. It was only on January 22, 1942, that the accused was informed by the Prime Minister that there had been children among the casualties at Novi Sad. He demanded an explanation from Feketehalmy-Czeydner, who denied this completely, and again depicted the local situation unrealistically to the accused.

General Szombathelyi categorically forbade cruelties in his telegram to the commander. The person in question, in spite of all this, and with the aim of arousing the battle spirit and lust for murder, organized an artificial guerilla fight that produced "wounded casualties". He ordered Mayor Miklós Nagy to supply the soldiers with tea spiked with rum, reasonimg that the weather was cold; blood and alcohol had their effect. The massacre continued in disastrous proportions; in January 1942, in Zabalj and Novi Sad, the total number of civilian corpse was 3,309, including 147 children and 299 aged people.

Feketehalmy-Czeydner continued denying the attrocities, even after the events at Novi Sad. The accused, according to his defense, believed him, because he would not expect such baseness from an old, well known army comrade. At any rate, he asked him for a written report. However, both his official and prosecutor's reports were uninformative. The official diaries of the army units did not contain any information either. He asked for a judicial enquiry, from these sources he could not gain a clear picture of the events. Altough the judicial enquiry entirely exposed the terrible atrocities of the soldiers, he presented a plea for barring the indictment to the Regent. The reason was that the politicians refused to back the case, and the German military attache implied, that Germany did not want a great affair made of the matter.

When the Kállay Government undertook the political clarification of the events in Bácska, the Regent ordered the reopening of the case, the accused entrusted a special court with the legal procedings. He appointed the members of the court with special care to guarantee the uncovering of the truth. He did not order the arrest of the principal criminals, in spite of the demands of his prosecutor, judge-advocate Mr. Babós. According to his defense, he did not believe that generals of high rank would escape. He trusted them even more, when Feketehalmy-Czeydner and Grassy announced how glad they were to be able to clear themselves of the unfounded accusations. These in question escaped after all with German help, and returned only after the German invasion of Hungary on March 19, 1944. They were reappointed to the corp of generals, plus there was an order barring indictment and a total rehabilitation.

The accused denied his guilt concerning the events in the South, though essentially he confessed to know the facts.

In connection with the statements of facts in the second article, the People's Court found reasons to believe, that the accused sent a telegram to Feketehalmy-Czeydner on January 22, 1942, saying that "striking injustices are to be avoided"; this cannot be confirmed. The pertinent part of Grassy's testimony cannot be accepted as substantial proof in itself, because the person in question cannot be regarded as an unconcerned party. What is more, he had been one of the central figures of the events. It is evident that he tried to exonerate himself by all possible means, and shift the responsibility at least partially upon somebody else.

According to the testimony of witness Imre Suhay, which he made on the basis of conscientious perusing the pertinent documents, there was no such telegram among the documents, *only telegram that forbid cruelties categorically.* Even if there had been such a telegram, it is sophistry to misinterpret it as a disguised instigation to permitt excesses. The killing of children is a "striking injustice" beyond doubt. The murdering of children would have been forbidden, even by the telegrammed order containing the prohibition. Such an instigation cannot be found even with the distortion of the meaning of the telegram.

In connection with the Southern events, the responsibility of the accused as either instigator, culprit or participant cannot be substantiated. According to the decisive statement of facts, the accused was informed of the massacre after it had taken place. This had been decided in relation with the verdict of the People's Court against Bárdossy. It is also true in the case of the accused, who learned of the events only from Bárdossy on January 22, 1942. Instigation, culpability or participation are thus out of the question. The telegram of the accused on January 22, 1942, cannot be regarded as instigation either, as it was settled above by the

Court.

The accused did not hurry to punish the criminals with the force he would have had to use, as it would have been his duty under such circumstances, since he had no doubt later of what had happened in the South. These events have influenced the nation's moral and also its financial existence. The question arose, are we going to become the object of hatred among the nations?

Under such circumstances, the accused put the investigation of the case in the hands of military leaders, whose impartiality would have been suspected by any sober outside observer. They were the most likely to have participated directly or indirectly in the scandalous operations. Instead of arresting those who were obviously responsible for the events as military commanders, the accused commissioned the principal criminal to undertake the enquiry. Before the watchful eyes and obvious disapproval of the international public opinion, he helped to cover up the case, which eventually led to the barring of the indictment. The problem was of such importance that not a moment of delay should have been allowed; old people and children had been murdered. There had been a "campaign" against them. In such an important case all other aspects are negligible. He ought to have struck instantly, thus making it clear, that the Hungarian government had no quarrel with the Serbs, was ready to support the minority not only with words but with action also. The cover-up of the case has been more harmful than advantageous.

There was no doubt about the series of crimes that took place. The punishment should have been immediate and with deterrent strength, as every sober and honest Hungarian and the whole world's public opinion expected it to be. It was evident that a treacherous clique opposed its own nation, some officers or gendarme commanders may commit such a crime, but the Hungarian nation and its government would not stand for it. It is the exposure, the complete openness in the handling of the case,that would have guaranteed a fair assessment of the tragedy in the Western public and official oppinion.

The glossing over and the attempted concealment of the case created the misconception that it had not been an arbitrary but tolerated course of action. It is well known what a great harm befell the Hungarians. The delayment of the case for weeks or months, degenerated into such an international scandal that its consequences burdened the Hungarian nation for a long time.

The judgement of the People's Court was, for those who were trying to cover up the crimes of some high ranking officers who later joined the German service. The welfare of these criminals was more important than the interests and reputation of the Hungarian nation.

He had the chance to take effective measures to punish the guilty. Instead he acted in an indecisive, harmful way. If he were hindered, should have resigned at once, proving that a responsible Hungarian soldier does not take part directly or indirectly in the cover-up of such crime.

The massacres at Zabalj and Novi Sad could have only been regarded as ordinary mass murders ordered by some individuals in the spot, and not the manifestation of official Hungarian policy. Measures should have been taken according to this. The People's Court denounced the procedure used, and also the accused as a participant.

The guilt of the accused is evident in the fact that even when he had a clear picture of the events in the South, he submitted a report to the regime, but pleaded for a cover-up. Even after reinstituting the legal procedures, he did not order the arrest of the accused principal criminals, providing them an opportunity to escape to Germany.

In the opinion of the People's Court, General Szombathelyi's deed involves the characteristics of the crime of dereliction of duty by an official, defined in the first paragraph of the Penal Code Article 478. As a government official, he abused his official authority with the purpose of exempting someone from lawful punishment. He neglected the fulfillment of his official duty by preventing the prosecution of criminals. The argument that politics necessitated this, or that he acted under German pressure, cannot justify his reprehensible participation in the cover-up of the case, and may be considered merely as a mitigating circumstance. The verdict was ten years imprisonment.

The People's prosecutor lodged an appeal against the verdict. The National People's Court changed the decision of the People's Court in May 22, 1946, and sentenced the late Chief of the General Staff to life imprisonment. It is worth quoting again from the reasons adduced, which judged Szombathelyi's attitude more strictly:

"It is essential to establish the responsibility of the accused in the events at Novi Sad.

It is impossible that a leader of the highest rank, concerned with an illegal action that took the lives of thousands which he could have prevented by intervening; may successfully refer to his accepting the repeated false reports of the murderers' instigators and the murderers themselves without criticism and control. He believed them at the time when the honourable public opinion of the whole country was scandalized by the committed dishonours. The comrades' reports were more convincing for him than the bloody facts.

Before the culmination of the atrocities in January 22, 1942, he sent a telegram to the leader of the massacre-called-raid with an order that the striking injustices are to be avoided. Grassy, one of the direct culprits related this determinedly, and the National Council does not find the People's Court's scepticism towards his confession reasonable, because the accused himself concedes on the 28th page of his remarks, that under the effect of Czeydner's report he may have sent such a telegram to him on January 22.

So even if at the time of ordering the Armed Forces and the commissioning of Grassy to lead the raid, it was far from the intentions of the accused, that these Armed Forces should carry out mass murders at Novi Sad. By the fact that he did not avoid the possibility of further murders with the cancelling of the whole operation; and that he did not order the most rigorous, objective enquiry; and did not draw the conclusions with the merciless exercising of his judicial power; he has become responsible both of the previous and the later unlawful acts.

The accused did not make use of his court against these murders, but commissioned the principal criminal, General Czeydner, whose reports seemed more powerful in his eyes than any proof. His unconditioned belief in the reliability of a general, originating from the military caste solidarity, brought the result of horrible death of thousands of innocent people including women and children.

Months later he initiated a court-martial against the murderers, but as early as August he had already stopped the proceedings against them. Some of them including Grassy, he put up for promotion regardless of the outcome of a possible trial. After eighteen months, submitting to outward pressure, he is forced to initiate the procedure again through his court. In spite of his prosecutors repeated proposal he denies the arrests and they all escaped to Germany, who may well be said to stand on the same level of morality. The accused commemorated the horrible crime in a melancholy officer's order of the day, regarding it this time as a national catastrophe. Up to that time, he had regarded the raid as the brave and heroic deed of the Hungarian soldier. This fundamental switch of conviction after eighteen months was due only to the murderers' escape .

All these facts concerning the accused, the National Council has already considered against him, and included them in the war crime defined under the first article of the P.C., paragraph 11. Although they do not share the characteristics of the direct action carried out with the purpose explicit in the quoted article, they were in connection with it. Originating from a uniform volition, the behaviour of the accused realized the war crime in some of its details was evaluated as belonging to the same ideological circle."

A Yugoslavian delegation, whose responsible jurist member was Dr. Vladimir Gavrilovics, solicitor from Novi Sad, exercised political pressure and referred it to the approaching peace-negotiations. They demanded the extradition of Ferenc Szombathelyi and the principal criminals, who were already condemned in the case of the raids at Novi Sad for the purpose of a local Yugoslavian legal proceedings.

This Vladimir Gavrilovics was the counsel of the wealthy Serb landowner and industrialist György Dungyerszky in Bácska. He was the man, who had rescued the Nabob's family in January 20, 1942, following an order by telephone from Novi Sad. He had taken them to Budapest, forgetting about his own family. He had not been warned of the imminent danger and all his relatives apart from his old father fell victim to the bloodshed. In the demand for the culprits, the thirst for direct revenge brought extraordinarily strong arguments, although they had already received their final verdict; the severest metted out. They argued that "The decision of the Hungarian judicial authorities will have influence on the outcome of the approaching peace negotiations!"

Obviously this has been one of the most important arguments that the Hungarian authorities yielded.

The victorious powers signed the peace treaty with the Hungarians or forced the treaty on the Hungarians at the Paris Peace Conference on August 24, 1946.

Our Foreign Minister, János Gyöngyösi, and the members of the Hungarian delegation made and expressed wishes only in relation with the population and territories of Czechoslovakia and Romania. There were no reproachful conclusions drawn against Yugoslavia, although the letter from Esztergom relating to the murder of 40-50 thousand Hungarians in Bácska was likely to have been in Gyöngyösi's pockets. They did not dare mention grievances of the invasion of North Torontál and North Bácska, both parts of the remnants of Hungary defined by Trianon in the 1920 Peace Treaty by Serbian partisan gangs without authority in September and October. This meant plundering, ransoming and kidnapping. On one occasion they forced their way into the railway station of Szeged with an armored train. After having plundered food and clothes, they returned with full wagons to Serbian territory.

The attack and indictment by the Yugoslavian "peace-delegate" in concern with the Peace Treaty with Hungary took place on August 24, 1946:

"Today we have started the debate of the Hungarian Treaty Proposal, said the Serb delegate, Edward Kardelj; I would like to relate the Yugoslavian delegation's viewpoint with some general remarks:

The Yugoslavian nations for centuries have been the victims of Hungarian feudal lords and chauvinists, who had been possessed by the idea of expansion for the creation of the St. Stephen's Crown's State. The St. Stephen's State was to expand to the Adriatic, which pursued a violent policy against our population, and backed all policies which aimed at the weakening of the Yugoslavian nations and states.

There are various forms of Hungarian assaults against the Yugoslavians, such as the subjugation and violent assimilation in the first centuries, when the Hungarians and the Yugoslavians got in touch on the Pannon Plateau. There had been the expansion of the regime on certain parts of Yugoslavian national territories; the policy that lasted through several centuries until the Turkish invasion. There had been the vehement and repeated pursuit of the Yugoslavians, their relocation and murder after the great defeat from the Turks. There was a policy of national oppression and permanent Magyarization with new methods in recent times, especially after the compromise of 1867 between Austria and Hungary. Horthy infected the Hungarian nation with revisionist ideas, who based its policy on the revival of the St. Stephen Empire."

The opening argument is abundant in blatant falsifications of history. In the beginning of our book, we related in accordance with historiography, that at the time of the Hungarian conquest, there was only a thin Bulgarian and Slavic population on the South Plain; the infiltration of Serbs was to come in the following centuries. It was especially the consequence of the northward-

bound expansion of the Turkish Empire. The Serbs had their rights, and demanded more and more of them; they suffered no violent assimilation.

"The Hungarian imperialists and chauvinists were incapable of accepting the borders fixed in the peace treaty of Trianon after World War I. They nursed permanent resentment and the spirit of revenge among the Hungarians in Yugoslavia against the Yugoslavians continued   Mr. Kardelj. For this reason the Hungarian leaders backed all the activities of fascist and terrorist forces, which aimed at the undermining of the Yugoslavian authority.

The Hungarian government eluded its responsibility ensuing from the Peace Treaty of Trianon, especially in concern with the flood-control system, cut off by the borders, which caused our population incalculable losses. Failure to fulfill these duties brought unfortunate consequences. The Danube and its affluents flooded the rich plains of Vojvodina, and changed the productive region into a swamp."

In Bácska the southern Slavs were in a minority at the time of the dictated peace at Trianon, not even reaching one-third of the population. The flood-control system, cut off by the borders damaged the Hungarian plain first, since all the rivers of Hungary spring from outside its borders. The accusation that Hungarian carelessness had turned the rich plains of Vojvodina into marshland is simply untrue, a political humbug.

"Horthy and his government's policy made Hungary a real storm-center of impatience in central Europe. Hungary joined the fascist states and obviously helped in the preparation for the fascist offensive, which demanded the martyrdom of freedom loving nations, said Kardelj.

The Horthy regime disloyally broke the Lasting Peace and Eternal Friendship Treaty, which it had signed with Yugoslavia on December 12,1940 and with Germany on April 3, 1941 which aimed at an offensive against Yugoslavia. The government put its territory at the German army's disposal to help the latter in its military operations against Yugoslavia."

The Serb delegate completely forgot the fact that the German military force had delivered an ultimatum to the Hungarian government, and that because of the forced breaking of the Eternal Friendship Treaty, Prime Minister Pál Teleki committed suicide.

155

There is no similar precedent in contemporary European diplomacy.

"At the time of the occupation, the Hungarian military forces and the Hungarian officials had committed an endless number of crimes against the Yugoslavian population. They had murdered 18,000 Yugoslavians in Bácska and harmed 104,000 people which means that 122,000 or 43% of the population became victims of the Hungarian terror. Every second Yugoslavian was killed or became a victim of violence in concentration camps during their imprisonment and internment. The Hungarian occupying forces committed such crimes in large numbers at Muraköz and Murántul. In spite of all fundamental decrees of international law, Hungary incorporated these Yugoslavian regions apart from Murántul, and relocated Bukovinian Hungarians there to change the ethnic character of the Yugoslavian lands for its own benefit."

There were unscrupulous falsifications in the exaggeration of the Hungarian Armed Forces' crimes. The official Yugoslavian data serves as up-to-date refutation: The official publication "Zlocini Skupstore u Vojvodini" Novi Sad 1946, which still exaggerates, mentions 6094 executed and 11,658 slandered Serbs. This is one-third and one-tenth of the peace delegate's agitative, false figures.

"The Hungarian Imperialists' Chauvinist and Revisionist Policy before the war had such a strong effect on some Hungarians in Yugoslavia, that they attended the service of the Hungarian Military Forces and the authority in occupation. They took part in many crimes, and corroborated with the invaders.

It is clear, that the Hungarian Fascists and Chauvinists roused impatience in this part of Europe, exciting hatred between the Yugoslavian nations and the Hungarians and causing murders.

However, Yugoslavia knows that there are democratic powers in Hungary today that are determined to break the relation with this awful past, these powers struggle for good neighborly relations with the Yugoslavian nation. The Yugoslavian delegation is led by the principles of a good-neighborly and friendly relationship with the Hungarian nation, when it presents a codicil for the Hungarian peace treaty proposal; and by the intention of supporting the Hungarian nation in the creation of a firm democratic system in its country. By no means, would it allow to be led by the principle of revenge against the Hungarians. For all

156

these reasons, it has minimized its demands for compensation for damages, the Hungarian occupation caused us, and the total cost of which is ten times the sum granted in the peace treaty proposal.

With our demands, we by no means want to aggravate the political and economical situation of Hungary as a defeated power, but we wish to help the country in its rapid progress. The Yugoslavian government is bound to exercise friendly politics with its neighbor; with the conviction that such a policy can only help the consolidation of democracy in Hungary, and the stabilization of peace in this part of Europe. The desperate struggle of the Hungarian democratic forces against those fascist remnants, which today tries to revive revisionism and aims at sowing the seed of the St. Stephen's Crown illusion show, that there are such democratic forces in Hungary. They do not allow the renewal of the imperialist policy so dear to the Horthy regime, and that may guarantee normal, firm and friendly relations with the neighbors."

The "peacemaker" Serb politician would have had an occasion to mention, after having multiplied the damage caused by the Hungarian reoccupation ten times, that the bloodshed by Hungarians had been revenged tenfold on the Hungarian population.

"The Yugoslavian delegation regards its demands from Hungary as bearing such characteristics that would deserve Hungary's sympathy and friendliness towards Yugoslavia. Since it wants to establish friendly relations with Hungary, Yugoslavia has not presented its territorial claims, though a significant number of the population belonging to Yugoslavia has remained on the other side of the border. We hope that the Hungarian government will respect the instructions of the peace treaty, and will guarantee freedom and equality for the Yugoslavians, ever more when it realizes that Yugoslavia has allowed freedom and equality for the Hungarians, like participation in the local administration. We have solved the problem of the relocation of the population on the grounds of free will, though a significant number of Hungarians live in Yugoslavia, who had severely hurt our nation with their hostile behaviour towards the population. We wish to live in peace and good friendship with Hungary. We have considered all the claims of Hungary in this respect, and have reduced our claims to the very minimum."

The Yugoslavian authorities had informed Foreign Minister Gyöngyösi at the very beginning of our democracy, that they plan to decrease the Hungarian population of Bácska by 40 thousand. In the course of the events, they probably have realized that the eviction of these 40 thousand souls had already taken place by simply murdering them......

FATAL COMEDY AT THE COURT OF JUSTICE

In the autumn of 1946, a short press report announced that the Hungarian government delivered Generals Ferenc Szombathelyi, Grassy, Feketehalmy-Zeidner, Captain Márton Zöldy and Nagy, the late mayor, as war criminals to Yugoslavia. We were convinced that they would not be content with their simple execution. In the Autumn of 1946, the population was informed in newspapers and through the radio, that the trials of the war criminals delivered to Yugoslavia will be organized in the theatre-hall of the "Dom Kultura", the late Cultural Centre. There was an open trial to which everyone would gain free admittance until the theatre hall was filled.

By the time the trial started, the group of the accused was enlarged. It was joined by Popovic, the Representative of the National Assembly in Bácska and Perepatic, merchant from Novi Sad, whose nickname was "cheap", which he was given for his advertisements displayed in the movies" stated György Szigeti in his memoirs.

"While the Hungarian officers were questioned about the raid, Popovic and Perepatic had to give account of their collaboration with the "Fascists during the occupation". They wanted to confiscate the huge property of the merchant

The late Lord Lieutenant, Péter Fernbach, was missing from the group of the accused, though everyone knew that the partisans had caught him. According to the spreading news, he was tortured to death in prison.

The judges assembling as a military court wore the uniform of the Titoist Army. The Public Prosecutor of Vojvodina, Dr. Gyetvai, the hangman of Hungarians levelled the charges.

Everyone was aware from the beginning, that the trial would end in a bloody comedy. They have to die whatever happens, because the court is not after the truth, but declares a death sentence prepared in advance. The only one who did not expect execution throughout the whole procedure was Perepatic, the merchant. It did not occur to him that his chief crime is his property.

The appointed public defense attorney acted as prosecutor. The accused were thrown prey to the Serb population of Curog and Zabalj, who supported the partisans. The Hungarians who had fled; who had survived the partisans revenge could not participate in the trial due to their innocence. The atmosphere of the trial grew dense from anti-Hungarian hatred. According to the practice of communist jurisprudence, not the prosecutor who was to prove the guilt of the accused, but the latter has to prove his innocence.

The district and the hall was full of militiamen and OZNA agents. During the trial the encouraging shout echoed in every fifth minute: "Na vesab snjima! Hang them!"

After a one week trial, the accused were all sentenced to death in the name of the people. Szombathelyi, Feketehalmy, Grassy and Zöldy were hanged, Popovic, Perepatic and Nagy were were shot. Execution by hanging was to be public. Szombathelyi and Zöldy were hanged in front of the Serb Cemetery at Novi Sad, called "Almaska Groblje". Feketehalmy was executed in Curog, Grassy in Zabalj."

The new Vajdasági Magyar Szó relates the statement of Ferenc Szombathelyi made by the right of the last word: "I do not feel guilty; my conscience is clear!" In spite of this the verdict pronounced on October 31, on the stage of the Cultural Centre was death for all the accused. Feketehalmy and Grassy scolded each other, Zöldy limped, which he had not done in the people's court of Budapest. According to the report of the Hungarian daily, Grassy and Zöldy were considered deserving of being hanged, and Szombathelyi of being shot. It seems as if the newspaper had forgotten about Feketehalmy-Czeydner.

There is some difference in the place and way of execution in the oral account we have. Grassy and Zöldy were hanged publicly in the end of Kiszacsi Street. The executions by shooting, including Szombathelyi's, according to the Vajdasági Magyar Szó - were carried out without an audience in the Fort of Pétervárad.

There are only unconfirmed reports today of the three generals execution; there were no known witnesses. These reports have been included in the memoirs of General Géza Lakatos, too. According to them, Ferenc Szombathelyi was impaled at Novi Sad. Feketehalmy at Curog and Grassy at Zabalj were buried in the ground alive up to the ears, and made even with the ground by a tank.

The Hungarian Department of Justice had delivered their guilty citizens to the Yugoslavians, on condition that the new sentence imposed on the condemned would not exceed the previous one in severity. This promise could have defended Szombathelyi, since his Hungarian sentence was only life imprisonment.

The Hungarian judicial authorities did not protest the "announcement" of the execution of their citizens.

Officially they did not even seem to have realized that the war criminals who had been extradited from the Western Allied Authorities the previous year or before had slipped from their province of authority of administering justice.

The People's Court of Budapest justified in a decree on February 25, 1947, that it accepts the definitive verdicts passed by the National People's Court and declared them enforceable. This means that it orders the beginning of life imprisonment for Szombathelyi.

INSTEAD OF AN EPILOGUE

Constantinus Porphyrogenitus wrote in the third part of his work: The **Governing** of the **Empire,** about the Southern Slavs: Xenophobia; hatred towards strangers is a general characteristic of their attitude. Are we justified in stating that even in the era of Porphirogenitus, the Hungarian conquerors had felt and behaved just the opposite? If our standard is in accordance with St. Stephen's **"Admonitions"**, we might be.

At the time of the Turkish army's advance to Esztergom, if not before, the Hungarians had learned the source of fear (often of horror). It is unlikely that all those bloody crimes described in previous chapters of this book, could be explained by some kind of mutual xenophobia. Political and military history can give a more general reason for such or genocide.

The Paris Peace Treaty that was forced on the country after the great defeat of the Austro-Hungarian Monarchy in World War I, has increased the Hungarian's fear and antipathy of all neighboring nations. The atmosphere of hatred and the *knowing* of being hated had been first of all due to the incredible injustice of one and a half million Hungarians who remained just outside the borders. In all of the bordering countries, the succession states had no need for them nor the two and a half million Hungarians further away from the new borders.

These countries in the course of seventy years have plainly made all-out efforts to clear the Hungarian dominated borderland of the Hungarians with all devices at their disposal peacefull or criminal..

Let us be content with Bácska this time. In comparison with the population of 1918, the number of Hungarians in the South has decreased by 170,000, while the so called "dominant population" (i.e. the Serbs) **has doubled or tripled.**

The Hungarian population of Bácska continues decreasing

nowadays as well. The last decade brought fewer births than deaths. In this respect, Bácska follows the trend of Hungary and even surpasses it in a way.

The sad habit of suicide surpasses the Fatherland.The number of "invited deaths" of the Hungarian minority exceeds the Yugoslavian average by a margin of 5 to 1 or 6 to 1. In Hungary the dark paradise of suicides are Csongrád and Bács-Kiskun counties. The Hungarians in the neighboring Szabadka exercise this kind of death at double that rate .

The whole Hungarian nation suffers in its heart from the wounds of the great defeats of the century. It not only feels defeated, but also cast to the mercy of its neighbors. These wounds are even fresher in the souls of Hungarians in Bácska.

During the last forty years the general attitude of the Hungarians in Bácska has been on the defensive and dominated by suffering; they live in fear, feel homeless. They feel they can not be the masters of their own fate; they are secondary citizens. Sooner or later they will be forced to give up their national identity, because the Serbian authority will not consider them as political factors.

When the intelligentsia speaks up as Hungarians, they are denounced as chauvinists, traitors. The severest form of oppression is the prohibition to speak about the last months of 1944. There is prohibition of commemoration and mourning, even though there is no manifestation of the intention of revenge by the Hungarians.

The crosses, the markers, the garlands, the flowers have all disappeared from the common graves. The tombs are used as garbage dumps, because the Balcanic pride of the governing Serb nation is unable to face the facts, that in the name of the "Yugoslavian nation" some blood thirsty criminals could have committed such abominable crimes.

Postscriptum

In 1941, the illegally settled Serb Dobrovoljacs, Serb Royalist Chetniks and Tito's Serb Partizans started the killings in Voivodina. Whoever starts guerilla warfare has to bear the responsibility and accept the consequences. **However, the victors are never prosecuted; the loosers are.**

Since the Vietnam war, we all know how the partisan forces are organized in any country; where the terrain is suitable for hit and run operations and provides good sanctuaries:

The Partisans start with a few tough guys, who have the killer instinct and originated from the village they are about to organize. They slip in during the night, wake up some men and tell them, that from now on they are part of the partisan unit and have to obey orders or else; few will resist. Those who do are killed on the spot, sometimes with the whole family watching. The word spreads fast about the punishment. From then on, nobody in his right mind would resist the "call to arms". During the day, most of them work in the fields like any other law-abiding citizen. At nightfall, they dig up their submachine guns and do what was ordered.

First they order a local boy to kill a sentry of the occupying force, a policeman or a village elder, on a dark, overcast night. They usually mutilate the body to make sure that the unfortunate victim's buddies get really mad at the unseen foe.

At this point, the commander of the occupying force orders an investigation. His angry men, out to avenge the gruesome death of their buddy, grab someone, who under duress, will confess to the heinous crime or accuse somebody else. In either case the fingered man either "resists arrest" and killed or "hangs himself". In "retaliation" the partisans get bolder and with local help, whole police detachments are annihilated.

From then on all hell breaks loose. The general fear and distrust takes over. In racially mixed villages, after living together in relative peace for hundreds of years, the animosity grows by the day. Eventually the situation gets out of hand; a junior officer or his men will start the indiscriminate killing.

This is the only reason for the partisan organization. The military effect of them in a densely inhabited, civilized country is negligible. A well placed, unarmed saboteur could inflict more damage on a military or industrial target than a ragtag partisan army ever could.

As a fighting force, Tito's partisans were totally ineffective when they came down from the mountains and were forced into the role of the infantry.

When the war ended, that was a different matter. They were set upon the unarmed civilians or disarmed soldiers. That is when the indiscriminate killing started on a truly wholesale and gruesome basis. They massacred Hungarians, Croatians, Germans and the Chetniks of General Mihailovits; their own kin, with equal abandon. They were true to their national character and communist indoctrination.

In Vietnam, the situation was different, but only to a certain extent. The terrain was excellent for hiding, booby trapping and ambushes. The populace was mostly homogeneous. The leadership of the Viet Kong knew that in "set piece battles", they didn't have a chance. So they followed the teachings of Mao ruthlessly and to the letter. The poor peasants had no choice; they were either killed by the Americans, or if they did not obey by the Viet Kong. Most of the 58,000 U.S. men killed in action were murdered by the peasants, who neither had the desire to kill nor to be killed. They would rather have lived in peace.....

The real war criminals were not the Hungarian Sergeant Kovacs in Vojvodina or the American Lieutenant Calley at My Lai, although nobody can condone the hideous crimes they have committed. We should not forget what they had to endure for months on end; not only the threat of instant death, which would have been salvation; but the very real possibility of being maimed for life; blinded or mutilated by a peasant girl who was forced in this mess by the horrible circumstances.

The real war criminals were not our fathers, brothers, sons, but Mao, Ho Si Minh, Stalin, Tito, and their henchmen, who coldly, premeditatedly forced this aberration on the human race.

CREDITS

Albert, Gábor: Emelt fővel. (With Head High)

A. Sajti, Enikő: Délvidék (Vojvodina)

Bajcsi-Zsilinszky E.: Helyünk és sorsunk Europában (Our Place and Fate in Europe)

Baky F.- Vebel L.: A Petőfi Brigád (The Petőfi Brigade.)

Brindza, Károly: Mondd el helyettem, elvtárs (Tell it for Me, Comrade.)

Burányi, Nándor: Összeroppanás (Collapse)

Buzasi, János: Az ujvidéki "razzia" (The Novi Sad "Raid")

Illés, Sándor: Sirató (Wailing)

Dalibor M. Krno: A békéről tárgyaltunk Magyarországgal (We Negotiated Peace with Hungary)

Matuska, Márton: 45 nap 44-ben. (45 Days in 44) Essays in the Magyar Szó, Novi Sad.

Sebestyén, Ádám: Andrásfalviak menekülése Bácskából (The Flight of the People of Andrásfalva from Vojvodina)

Sára, Sándor: Keresztúton (On Crossroads)

Szigethy, György: Szemtanuja voltam Tito délvidéki vérengzéseinek. (I was an eyewitness of Tito's Bloodshed in Vojvodina).

Szombathelyi, Ferenc: Visszaemlékezései 1945 (Remembrances, 1945)

Szőcs M. - Kovács J.: Halottak hallgatása (Silence of the Dead)

Jovan Veselinov Zsarko: Az autonom Vajdaság születése (The Birth of the Autonomous Vojvodina)

165

Recommended reading;

Rudolf Kiszliong; "The Croaten: Der Schicksalsweg eines Suedslawenvolkes", Graz-Koeln, 1956

John Pecola and Stanko Guldescu; "Operation Slaughterhouse: Eyewitness Accounts of Postwar Massacres in Yugoslavia". Philladelphia, 1970

Andre Ott; "Dangers Serbes sur la Croatie", Paris, 1982

Nicolai Tolstoy; "The Minister and the Massacres", London, 1986

Joseph Hecimovic; "In Tito's Death Marches", New York, 1992

Wendelin Gruber: "In den Faengen des Roten Drachen" Miriam Verlag, Munich.

TABLE OF CONTENTS

Authors Preface 9
Historical Antecedents 12
Cold Days. A Novel and a Film 18
Vendetta. Retaliation Multiplied 19
People of Bezdan 22
Ujvidek, Renamed Novi Sad 50
Szentamas - Foldvar 59
Adorjan; Nadirjan, The Unfortunate 67
Kanizsa 74
Obecse and Veronica's Veil 76
Early Partisans With Lili-White Hands 78
From Szentfulop To The Gakova Camp 82
Temerin 86
Horgos, Martonos, Zenta 91
Ada - The Bridge Of Life. Mohol - Death For Land 99
Peterreve. Csurog: Till The Last Hungarian 103
Zsablya 109
Death Of The Punters. 111
Mozsor, Zombor, Verbasz, Pacser, Bajmok 116
Szabadka, Apatin - Kula 123
Where There Was A Reconciliation 129
The Szekelys Run The Gauntlet 130
The Petofi Brigade 133
Report of Losses 137
Verdicts After Revenge 142
Fatal Comedy At The Court Of Justice 158
Instead Of An Epiloge 160
Postsriptum 162
Credits 164
Recommended Reading 165

Books of Interest on Hungary and East-Central Europe

AUTHOR	TITLE
Baross, Gabor	Hungary and Hitler
Bogdan, Henry	From Warsaw to Sofia
Borsody, Stephen	The New Central Europe
Borsody, Stephen ed.	The Hungarians. A Divided Nation
Cadzow, Ludanyi, Elteto	Transylvania. The Roots of Ethnic Conflict.
Chaszar, Edward	Decision in Vienna.
	The Czechoslovak-Hungarian Border Dispute
Chaszar, Edward	The International Problem of National Minorities
Chaszar, Edward	International Protection of Minorities:
Cseres, Tibor	Titoist Atrocities in Vojvodina 1944-1945
DuNay, Andree	The Early History of the Rumanian Language
Hogye, Michael	The Last Satellite?
	Hungary's Destiny at the End of WW.II
Illyes, Elemer	National Minorities in Romania.
	Change in Transylvania.
Illyes, Elemer	Ethnic Continuity in the Carpato-Danubian Area
Janics, Kalman	Czechoslovak Policy and the Hungarian Minority.
	War & Society, etc. Vol. IV.
Kertesz, Stephen D.	The Last European Peace Conference
Kertesz, Stephen D.	Between Russia and the West.
	Hungary and the Illusion of Peacemaking.
Kiraly, Pastor, Sanders	Total War and Peacemaking.
	A Case Study of Trianon. War & Society, Vol. IV
Kostya, Sandor	Northern Hungary.
	A Historical Study of the Chechoslovak Republic
Kosztin, Arpad	The Daco-Roman Legend
Lote, Louis L. ed.	Transylvania
Major, Mark imre	American-Hungarian Relations 1918-1944
Montgomery, John F.	Hungary the Unwilling Satellite
Romsics, Ignac ed.	Wartime American Plans for a New Hungary
Sakmyster, Thomas L.	Hungary, the Great Powers and
	the Danubian Crisis, 1936-1939.
Szent-Ivanyi	Janos Esterhazy
	(A Hungarian Leader in Czechoslovakia)
T.V.F. & Danubian R.	Genocide in Transylvania
Wagner, Frances S.	Toward a New Central Europe
Wagner, Frances S.	Hungarian Contributions to World Civilisation
Wojatsek, Charles	From Trianon to the First Vienna Award.